My Thorns Formed My Crown

YOUR TRAUMA GIVES BIRTH TO YOUR PURPOSE

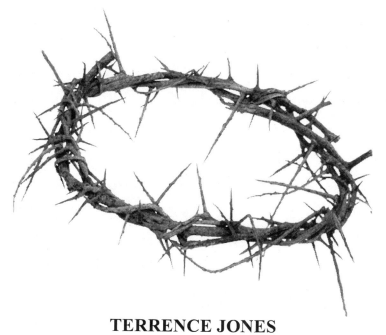

TERRENCE JONES

My Thorns Formed My Crown:
Your Trauma Gives Birth To Your Purpose
Copyright © 2011
Terrence Jones

Edited by Tiffani Staten and Terrence Jones
Cover design by Vanzago Johnson

ISBN: 978-0-615-51169-6

Library of Congress Control Number: 2011912174

All Scripture quotations are taken from the **KING JAMES
VERSION** of the Bible, unless otherwise indicated.

Scripture quotations marked *NASB* are taken from the
NEW AMERICAN STANDARD BIBLE®, Copyright © 1960,
1962, 1963, 1968, 1971, 1972, 1973, 1975, 1977, 1995 by The
Lockman Foundation. Used by permission.

Scripture quotations marked *The Message* are taken from
THE MESSAGE, Copyright © by Eugene H. Peterson 1993, 1994,
1995, 1996, 2000, 2001, 2002. Used by permission of NavPress
Publishing Group.

For ordering information, please visit
www.tjonesspeaks.com.

Printed in the USA by
Morris Publishing®
3212 E. Hwy. 30 · Kearney, NE 68847
800-650-7888 · www.morrispublishing.com

This book is dedicated with love
in memory of my mother
Betty Ann Jones

"It is the glory of God to conceal a thing: but the honour of kings is to search out a matter."

-Proverbs 25:2

Table of Contents

Introduction   7

1st Quarter: The Causes of Trauma
  1. In the Beginning there was Trauma   11
  2. My Elementary Years   17
  3. The Dead Season   27
  4. Do or Die Junior High   31
  5. Self-Worthlessness   39

2nd Quarter: The Affects of Trauma
  6. Hopeless High School Years   47
  7. The Dark Files   57
  8. Pain   67
  9. The Shadow of Death   73
  10. Adversity   77
  11. Well Done Mama   85

Half-Time: Reflection and Recovery
  12. Reflection: Understanding the Past   97
  13. Recovery: Unearthing Your Purpose   101

3rd Quarter: Road to Recovery
  14. New Wine   107
  15. Boot Camp   117
  16. Therapy: Get Your Mind Right   127

4th Quarter: The Blessings and Purpose of Trauma
  17. Our Fathers   137
  18. Wheat and Weeds   147
  19. Jesus of the Hood   153
  20. Piece of Bread   161
  21. Principalities and Personalities   169
  22. Life Lessons In Death   177
  23. Character   183
  24. Evergreen   197
  25. My Crown   209

Epilogue   219
Works Cited   223

Introduction

Upon reading the title and seeing the crown of thorns on the cover, you may have concluded that this book is about pain and suffering. If you're anything like me, you probably said to yourself, "I got my own problems, so why would I want to read about somebody else's? I would much rather read something that is uplifting and inspirational." I understand, so I commend you for even taking the time and braving the waters to read this book.

To be perfectly honest with you, this book is about pain and suffering, but it's also about persevering and overcoming as well. Throughout the course of your life you will experience many trials and tribulations. However, what's truly uplifting and inspirational, is witnessing the lives of those who have battled and conquered every test and trial set before them. Therefore, if you truly want to be inspired, then this is the book for you.

Throughout the course of my life, I've experienced many traumatic events that had imprisoned me and kept me from achieving my fullest potential. Due to the pain and suffering that I witnessed and experienced, I developed a negative perspective on life and God. This mindset led me down a path of destruction.

Despite my calloused soul and reckless lifestyle, God intervened and snatched me from the jaws of hell. Not only did God save me but He transformed my mind and allowed me to see that He used the hell that I went through to equip me for a greater purpose.

In the following pages, I will take you on a journey of my life detailing the events that led me away from God and then eventually led me back to God. It is my hope that this book will inspire you to take a second look at the traumatic events that have transpired in your life and see that God used them to prepare you for greatness.

By the way, I am a Christian but there is some rather graphic language on some of the pages that follow; so if you are one of those "holier than thou" people who are so offended by anything that you consider to be unspiritual then put this book back on the shelf. But for those, like myself, who realize that we are all sinners in need of deliverance; please keep reading.

CAUTION! You're going to experience some major turbulence in the first half of this book, but I promise, things will get a whole lot better in the second half, so hang in there. Buckle up, because you're about to go for a ride.

1st Quarter:

The
Causes
of
Trauma

1

In the Beginning there was Trauma

Trauma: *1. a. a body wound or shock produced by physical injury, as from an accident. b. the condition produced by this. 2. Psychiatry. psychological shock or severe distress from experiencing a disastrous event outside the range of usual experience, as rape or military combat. 3. any wrenching or distressing experience, esp. one causing a disturbance in normal functioning.*

-Random House Webster's College Dictionary

JUST A NEWBORN

Pneumonia

From the time I was born, I had to struggle to survive. I developed pneumonia in both of my lungs when I was two months old. The doctors told my parents to give me cold baths to reduce the fever. My mother couldn't do it because it was too painful for her. My father said that I would scream at the top of my lungs when he put me in that cold water. This went on for several months. By the time I turned one year old, my medical records were thicker than a person's records that were in their twenties. This is how I came into the world; weak and sickly.

2 YEARS OLD

Gone to Church

Even though I was only two years old, I can remember this incident like it happened yesterday. One Sunday morning I woke up and my parents were gone. My father had taken my mother to church and left me in the apartment alone. I was scared to death. I got on my horse and started riding. When my dad got home he saw me crying and screaming as I was riding the horse. I have been scared to be alone ever since to some degree.

3 YEARS OLD

The Back Room

I was in Memphis, Tennessee at my grandmother's house. There was a room at the back of the house where the door constantly stayed shut. One day when my grandmother went into the room I followed behind her and I saw this woman lying on a bed. It was one of my grandmother's sisters, Aunt Katie.

When my grandmother took the sheets off of her I saw that she had sores all over her body that were dripping with blood. She was in so much pain that she couldn't move. She died not too long after that. All I can remember of Aunt Katie is me staring at her feeling helpless. It was creepy in that back room. To this day when I visit my grandmother's house, I don't like going into that back room.

4 YEARS OLD

The Big Bad Wolf

I was upstairs in my room playing with my toys and I heard my parents downstairs arguing as usual. Then all of a sudden, I heard some banging noises and then the yelling stopped. I went down stairs to see what was going on and I saw my father on top of my mother choking her. Her face was red and I saw that she couldn't breathe. I was so scared that I couldn't move.

When my father looked up and saw me, he let her go and walked out of the house. He slammed the door so hard it made the house shake. My mother was still lying on the floor coughing and crying. Terrified with tears running down my eyes and unable to move, I asked my mother was she alright and she said, "Terrence just go upstairs". Retreat became the norm. I was scared to death of my father ever since then.

Kindergarten

First year of school in Kindergarten and I was severely shy and withdrawn. I didn't have any brothers or sisters that lived with me and I didn't have any family in the area, which led to me being on my own most of the time. The only person that I spent time with was my mother because my father spent most of his time at work or hanging out in his hometown, Baltimore, MD. Therefore, my social skills were limited.

The kids in my class were rowdy and I was too scared to mix it up with them. My teacher tried to get me to interact with the other kids but was unsuccessful. She even called my parents to express her concern about how withdrawn and intimidated I was versus the other children in her class. She suggested that my parents hold me back and allow me to start school the following year. My parents disapproved and left me in school.

5 YEARS OLD

Punching Bag

As a result of my lack of testicular fortitude, it wasn't long before the other kids started picking on me. Wherever I went, I got ridiculed and beat up. I got beat up at school, at daycare, and even in my own neighborhood. Even the people who got bullied by other kids bullied me. I was at the very bottom of the food chain. The more I tried to mind my own business and keep away from people to avoid trouble, the more they made it their business to beat me up. I just couldn't understand why everyone targeted me. What was even worse was that girls were even making fun of me. I began to hate myself for being such a punk.

One of the main reasons I didn't fight back was due to my size. I was short and skinny. Many of the other kids my age were huge and I was much smaller than they were, so I figured there was no need for me to try and defend myself because I couldn't beat them anyway. Furthermore, many of the other kids had older siblings and other family members that would take up for them but I didn't have anybody. I was on my own.

My First Companion

When I was 5 years old, one of my father's friends gave us a red Doberman Pincher that we named, Major. I was too young to train the dog and my dad didn't take any time with him; so Major just spent his entire life running around the back yard.

A couple of months after we got the dog my father purchased a boat from a friend of his that he stored in the back yard. One day after my parents and I arrived at home my father saw Major in the backyard chewing something on his boat. When he went in the backyard to investigate he realized that Major had chewed up the entire gas line.

The next thing I know, my dad went in the house and got a broom stick and beat the hell out of Major. Major ran into his dog house and my dad stuck the broomstick in the dog house and kept on beating him. He was beating Major so bad that you could hear him yelping down the street. The next day when I went outside Major had a knot in the middle of his head. The knot never completely went down and it stayed on his head for the rest of his life. That knot looked like something from the cartoons.

Goodbye Granddad

In 1982, my grandfather died from a stroke. This was the first funeral that I can remember attending but far from the last. I have a very vivid memory and what branded the memory of this funeral in my mind for the rest of my life was my grandmother at my grandfather's casket screaming his name, "Pram, Pram, Pram!" I didn't really understand what death was back then and I just kept thinking to myself, "*Why isn't Granddad moving?*"

He didn't look the same in that casket. He was a whole lot darker. Nobody looks the same in their caskets. It was a very sad time and I began to dread death after that. Although my grandmother carried on after the passing of my grandfather, I could tell that she was never truly happy after that. How could she be, she had lost her soul mate. Death changes things and it seemed to me that it changes things for the worse.

CONCLUSIONS

1. They must not love me. If they did, then why did they leave me?
2. It is better to retreat than to fight back.

3. Nobody likes me. So I need to just keep to myself.
4. I am too little to stand up to anybody.
5. Don't mess with dad or his stuff because he will beat the hell out of you.
6. Death takes people away forever.

My Elementary Years

...a child's feelings are so strong that they cannot be repressed without serious consequences. The stronger a prisoner is, the thicker the prison walls have to be, and unfortunately these walls also impede or completely prevent later emotional growth. (58)

-Alice Miller, The Drama of the Gifted Child

6 YEARS OLD

You Hurt My Knuckles

I managed to survive Kindergarten and make it to the first grade. My first grade teacher used to wear dresses, as most female teachers did back in those days. This particular teacher was extremely mean and when you acted up in her class she would grab your hand, spread your fingers and hit your knuckles with this thick paint brush that she kept in her desk drawer.

Whenever she would approach one of the kid's desks to help them with their work the boys in the class would kneel down and look up her dress. At that time in my life I was a straight nerd and I found it rather appalling for those boys to do that. So what did I do? I broke rule number one, I snitched. I told the teacher that they were looking up her dress and she looked at me and said; "You probably were doing it too." I said, "No I wasn't." But she didn't believe me and after that I was on her radar. I couldn't believe that she didn't believe me and that she called me a liar.

Sometime later, I can't remember what I did, but it was extremely insignificant but because she thought I had looked up her dress, she pulled out her paint brush and tore my little knuckles up. Everybody in the class laughed at me and I went back to my seat and started crying. I could barely write after that. I was a very sensitive kid and I internalized that incident. I hated her for that. That's when I began to dislike school teachers and I figured what's the use of being good if I'm going to get into trouble anyway.

Reverend Ronald McDonald

I survived yet another pulverizing year of school and passed to the second grade. Ms. Smith, who was my second grade teacher had given us a homework assignment, which was to write about a particular African American Social Activist during those times. She gave us the name of the person she wanted the class to write about (let's just say his name was Reverend Ronald McDonald) and told us to have our parents help us with the assignment. At that time I had no idea who Reverend Ronald McDonald was, but, when I got home and told my parents about the assignment, my father went ballistic. He said (and I quote),

> *"Hell no, we ain't gonna sit here and right no goddamn paper about no goddamn Reverend Ronald McDonald. He ain't shit and he ain't done shit for our people. He is a goddamn glory hound. Give me that goddamn paper."*

He then proceeded to write the teacher a letter explaining why he didn't like Reverend Ronald McDonald and how he didn't appreciate her teaching us about him instead of teaching us about people like Dr. Martin Luther King, Jr. After my father completed his version of my homework assignment, he instructed me to turn it into the teacher and to inform her that if she had any questions to give him a call.

When the teacher read my homework she called another teacher and the school janitor into the classroom and had them read the letter as well. After reading the letter they just stared and pointed their fingers at me while they whispered to themselves. I was so embarrassed. Needless to say, she didn't call my father about my homework. I don't recall what grade I received on that assignment but I don't think it was good.

My Only Friend

One day when I was outside playing in my neighborhood, some boys beat me up real bad and chased me home. This was typical.

When I got home, my mother came outside and started yelling at them. She asked them, "Why do y'all keep picking on my son? All he wants to do is to be friends with y'all." Then she took me into the house.

Like I said this was normal but for some strange reason on this day I couldn't stop crying. I then said to my mother, "Ma, why do they hate me? I just want to be friends with them. Everybody hates me." She said, "Baby don't worry about them and that's not true, everybody doesn't hate you, because I love you and I'll always be your friend."

Dr. King

My father's job had sent him to Springfield, Massachusetts for a year and my mother and I were home alone. During that time in January they aired this movie about Dr. King and I sat down and watched the entire movie by myself from beginning to end.

At the end of the movie when they showed Dr. King's assassination, I couldn't stop crying. My mother couldn't calm me down so she called my father and had him talk to me. He explained to me that Dr. King was a great man and that he did a lot to help our people. What he said to me made me feel better. After I got off of the phone with him I told my mother, "Ma, I want to be like Dr. King. I want to help people." She replied, "Baby one day you will."

Uncle Lawrence

In 1984, one of my father's younger brothers died. His name was Uncle Lawrence. I don't remember too much about him but from what I heard he was a very angry and violent man. He was only about 5'-7" tall and weighed about 120 lbs. Despite his small stature, people were scared to death of him. His reputation preceded him wherever he went.

My father was extremely hurt because this was the first time he had to bury one of his brothers. My mother shared with me that she was scared of Uncle Lawrence and felt uncomfortable in his presence. Later on in my life when I really began to get into trouble my mother told me that I reminded her of my Uncle Lawrence.

It is a real mystery how he died, they say that one night while he was hanging out with his buddies drinking he passed out and when the ambulance finally arrived he had gone without oxygen for too long. They took him to the hospital and put him on life support. After a couple of days the family decided to take him off of life support and he died. He was only in his mid-forties.

8 YEARS OLD

Shoe Box Design

When I was in the third grade, I took the initiative and did a shoe box design with dinosaurs for extra credit. The next day I took it to school and gave it to my teacher and she told me that the only way I would receive the extra credit was to present it to the class. I said okay and during my presentation all of the kids booed and made fun of me. They called me a nerd and a teacher's pet. Everybody started laughing at me and I went back to my seat with my head down.

I didn't do anymore extra credit projects after that. I was too embarrassed and I wasn't willing to experience that type of rejection again despite the fact that I was a creative person. Later on I began to act up in class and started getting into trouble. Teachers started calling my house telling my parents that I was a troublemaker. Even though my grades were good sometimes I would fall short of the honor roll because of my behavior grade, which was usually a "D".

But I Got the Ball

My mother and father both worked full-time jobs, so after school I had to go to daycare. Over the course of my life, I have been to several different daycares and I hated them all because my parent's used to get off of work late and I was always the last kid to get picked up. There was this one particular daycare provider that my parents sent me to named, Ms. Johnson. She was mean as hell but she had her favorites and I wasn't one of them. I was a really shy kid and pretty much kept to myself so I had no idea why she didn't like me. Two of her favorite boys were Charlie and Harvey.

One day she let me, Charlie, and Harvey go to the elementary school to play baseball and she also let us use her oldest son's baseball. She stressed that she wanted us to bring it back because it belonged to her son and he would be upset if we lost it.

It was wintertime and there was a creek near the field behind the school where we were playing. It had just snowed and it was so cold outside that the creek had frozen. While we were playing, Charlie hit the ball and it landed on the creek. I said that he had to go get it because Ms. Johnson was going to have a fit if we didn't come back with that ball. Both of them were scared to go out on the ice and get the ball so they said to leave it.

The reason why they didn't care about getting the ball was they knew that they were not going to get in trouble and that she would most likely fuss at me. So to save myself from getting in trouble, I walked out on the ice to get the ball. When I reached the ball the ice broke and I fell in the creek. My pants were soaked and I was shivering as we walked all the way back to Ms. Johnson's house.

When we got back to Ms. Johnson's house she immediately started yelling at me about my clothes being wet. She picked me up and put me on this table and took my wet pants off to hang them up to dry. Then in front of all of the kids she said, "I should put a baby pamper on you." All of the kids started laughing, including Charlie and Harvey. I was so embarrassed because I had to sit there on that table in my underwear. I tried to defend myself by saying, "But Ms. Johnson I got your son's baseball." That didn't make a difference to her and she kept fussing. That's when I realized that I was damned if I do and damned if I don't.

9 YEARS OLD

Get Off Me

For numerous reasons, my mother had to keep switching my daycare providers. By far the worst place I had been to was Ms. Wesley's. Ms. Wesley had over seventy children in her basement. She more than exceeded the limit of children a daycare provider could service. She kept her operation hidden and she used her entire family (mother, sister, and daughters) to run her daycare while she spent most of her time shuttling children from school to her house.

Her basement stayed crowded. She had one room with a television and only their favorites were allowed to go into that room and watch cartoons. The other kids had to sit in the waiting room area on a bench until their parents came to pick them up. Of course, I was one of those kids who had to sit on the bench. We would normally spend four to five hours sitting on the bench after school doing nothing but waiting. One day I was talking too loud in the waiting room and Ms. Wesley's sister grabbed me in my collar and told me to shut up before she whipped me. I hated that place.

On occasion, Ms. Wesley's daughters who were seven to eight years older than I was would come into the waiting room and flirt with the young boys. Sometimes they would sit on my lap and kiss on me and tell me how cute I was. One of them was ugly as could be and she was the main one who would constantly harass me and tell me that I was her little boyfriend.

Whenever I saw her coming I felt like I was going to throw up. I was too scared of her to tell her to stop and to get off me because I feared that they would whip me. I begged my mother to find me another daycare provider and eventually she did. I never told her what the girls did to me, I just told her that I hated that place.

Baby Brother

On July 3, 1986 my baby brother was born. When I looked at him and held him in my arms for the first time I hated myself because I was a coward and wasn't worth looking up too. How could I be somebody's big brother when I myself was getting picked on? How could I inspire him to take up for himself and gain respect when I didn't have any myself? I realized right then and there that eventually I was going to have to make a change, if not for me then at least for my brother.

10 YEARS OLD

Major, Get Up

One day my Doberman Pincher, Major, collapsed in front of me. We had taken him to the veterinarian a few days prior because we could tell that he was sick and he was diagnosed with heartworms.

We hadn't taken care of him like we should have and even though the veterinarian gave him a 50/50 chance on surviving, my dad decided to go ahead and have him treated anyway. After a couple of days of treatment he looked a lot better so we were able to bring him home. I thought that he was going to pull through.

When he collapsed in front of me I was stunned because I could see him gasping for air. I called his name and he tried to get up and walk to me but he just collapsed again. I ran upstairs and got my dad. When we got back downstairs, Major had died. I couldn't stop crying. My dad went and sat on the step and put his head down. When I looked at him, I realized that he was crying too. I had never seen my father express any real emotion before besides anger. That was the first time I ever saw him cry. I didn't know what to do and I felt real uncomfortable.

Too Small

From time-to-time, I played football with the older kids in my neighborhood. One day during the kick off return they gave the ball to me and I took off running. Everybody was outside cheering me on screaming, "Go little Terrence," and when I looked back I had outran everybody. I was only ten years old but I was so fast that I had even outrun the teenagers.

Then it happened, just when I turned to look back, I ran slam into a parked van. The next thing I know, people were pulling me from under the van. The whole neighborhood was laughing. My knee was busted up and blood was all over my sweatpants. My glory was short-lived. I was so embarrassed.

Later on, a couple of the guys in my neighborhood started playing football for the local Boys Club and said that I should play because of my speed. I asked my dad to sign me up but he said no because I was too small and I would get hurt. I internalized that comment and from that moment on I became self-conscious about my size.

Field Day

In elementary school we had this event every year called, Field Day. The teachers would set the field up with all types of track and field events and the kids would compete against each other and the winners would be awarded prizes at the awards ceremony later on in the year.

I loved field day because I was naturally athletic and this was one of the only times that I got any positive recognition from people, especially my dad. You only competed against the kids at your grade level and I would always win first place in the fifty-yard dash, pull-ups, long jump, and the other individual activities. I dominated Field Day from kindergarten up until my fifth grade year.

In my sixth grade year my physical education teacher told me that she was assigning me to be a team captain for Field Day. I told her I didn't want to do it and she said, "Too bad." I was upset because I was scared to lead a team and it would also cause me to be responsible for other people and not be able to focus my attention on my individual performance.

When Field Day arrived, my team took the field and I turned into my dad. I was yelling and fussing at people, telling them to give me one more pull-up or you can run faster than that. By the time the day was over, I didn't get a chance to really perform the way I wanted to in the events that I normally excelled at and from what I saw my team didn't perform well either. I was crushed because the only thing that I looked forward to every year was bringing my awards home to show my father but it looked like this year I wasn't going to get any. I felt like a loser.

11 YEARS OLD

I'm Walking

Every daycare provider I went to posed a different type of challenge for me. I was either getting verbally or physically abused, neglected, molested, bullied, teased, you name it, I experienced it. I got fed up and one day after school let out, I didn't go to my daycare provider, instead I just walked home. I was only eleven years old but I walked over a mile all by myself.

When my mother found out she was extremely upset because she was afraid that someone would attack me or I would be kidnapped. I told her that I would take my chances with the kidnappers but I was not going back to the daycare. She realized that I had made up my mind and she said okay. It was scary walking home by myself but not scarier than the daycares.

CONCLUSIONS

1. It doesn't pay to tell the truth.
2. My dad is crazy as hell.
3. My mom is the only person who really cares about me.
4. I am going to help people one day.
5. I want to be tough like Uncle Lawrence.
6. There is no need to be creative and try something new.
7. It doesn't pay to do the right thing because I'm going to get in trouble regardless.
8. Don't tell on them because they will just hurt you even more the next time.
9. I am not worthy to be somebody's big brother.
10. You only cry if somebody or something dies.
11. I am too little and frail to play any physical sports.
12. I am not a leader.
13. I'm better off on my own because people who are supposed to take care of me keep on hurting me.

3

The Dead Season

Some people are so afraid to die that they never begin to live.

-Henry Van Dyke

9 YEARS OLD

Little Derrick

Every summer my parents would send me to stay with my grandmother in Memphis, Tennessee. One summer, one of the young local boys drowned in a swimming pool. His name was Derrick. I had never met him but it was customary for everyone in town to go to funerals, especially the funeral of a young child. Derrick was about a year older than I was.

My whole family walked around to view Derrick in his casket. He looked spooky to me. He was real dark and his skin was wrinkled and dry. His body was swollen and extremely stiff and his lips were real puffy. He didn't look anything like his pictures. Then all of a sudden people started screaming and crying and many of them had to be carried out. I became really scared and I wanted to leave but I couldn't because I had to stay with my grandmother.

Later on, I was so scared that I couldn't sleep with the lights off because I thought that Derrick was in the room and was going to get me. I have been terrified of dead people ever since.

10 YEARS OLD

Uncle Jack

I only met Uncle Jack one time and from what my dad tells me he was my father's favorite uncle. My father said that when he was young he wanted to be like Uncle Jack. Uncle Jack had plenty of money and plenty of women. When he died, my father took me and my mother to the funeral with him. I will never forget it. When I walked into the funeral home there were open caskets all over the room with dead bodies in them. The only way to get to Uncle Jack's funeral service was to walk through the room with all of the open caskets. I thought that those dead people were going to get up out of their caskets and grab me. I stood real close to my mother the entire time I was there.

I don't know why, but I never told my parents how scared I was. I couldn't sleep in the dark after that and I had to leave my television on as I slept at night because I believed that all of those dead people were going to come and get me. Sometimes I would even be so scared that I couldn't fall asleep until the sun came up. I began to associate darkness with death and light with safety.

11 YEARS OLD

Uncle Bo

Uncle Bo was another one of my father's younger brothers and he died from a heart attack. He was known to use heroine from time-to-time, which may have contributed to his death. I attended his funeral as well. My father was grief stricken by the loss of his brother because my father was one of the oldest siblings and he helped to raise his younger brothers. I believe that he felt responsible for how their lives turned out although he shouldn't have because he was their brother and not their father.

One day after the funeral, my father was in his room sleeping and while he slept he began to dream about Uncle Bo. I knew he was dreaming about Uncle Bo because as he slept I heard him yelling Uncle Bo's name. This scared the hell out of me but I woke my dad up and told him what was happening. I thought that Uncle Bo was haunting him and that he would also come to haunt me.

Uncle Eddie

When my mother's uncle, Uncle Eddie died, I became very sad because he was like our grandfather. I remember my grandmother screaming his name at his funeral as well. When I saw him in his casket he was a lot darker too, just like my grandfather. Despite how compassionate Uncle Eddie was to me and to everyone that he came in contact with, I still had nightmares that he was coming to get me after I saw him in the casket. My mind became twisted. I was terrified of death.

Madea

During the summer of 1988, I went to visit my mother's side of the family in Memphis, Tennessee. We had come to find out that my grandmother (Madea) had developed lung cancer and had been taking chemotherapy treatments. After my parents left to go back to Maryland Madea sat down at the kitchen table and took off her scarf. What I saw after that had me frozen like a deer caught in headlights. She didn't have any hair on her head. It had all fallen out as a result of the chemotherapy. I just stared at her and wanted to cry but I didn't because I didn't want to cry in her face.

At the end of the summer, my parents came to pick me up and take me home. When my mother kissed Madea goodbye, Madea began to cry uncontrollable. My mother began to console her and told her that we would be back for Christmas. At that time I didn't understand why Madea wouldn't stop crying. Madea died a week later. That's when I realized why she couldn't stop crying because she knew that would be the last time that she saw us. My mother was heart broken and so was I.

This was also the second time that I saw my father cry. Our family has never been the same since losing Madea because she kept everybody in line. By this time I was so afraid of dead people that I stood about ten feet away from Madea's casket at the funeral. Just like all of the other people I saw in caskets, she had gotten a whole lot darker. After her death, I was afraid to even stay in her house by myself. Death had me scared of my own grandmother.

CONCLUSIONS

1. Dead people will come back to haunt you.
2. You only cry when someone or something dies (reinforced).

4

Do or Die Junior High

Why are so many youth turning to violence against others or themselves? Many therapists point to the statistics that show that many youth perpetrators of violence are also victims of it...Children are exposed to violence not only within their homes but also in the outside world. Among children living in high-crime neighborhoods, more than one-third have witnessed a homicide by the time they turned 15 (Bell, 1991; Garbarino, 1995). A study of first and second graders living in Washington, DC, revealed that 45% had witnessed a mugging, 31% had witnessed a shooting, and 39% had seen a dead body (Cooley-Quille, Turner, & Beidel, 1995). In Chicago, since 1974, there has been a 400% increase in the rate of serious assaults that occur in public places. The conditions in cities like DC and Chicago are mirrored throughout the United States. More than 70% of high school students report that they have witnessed a serious assault and 40% of robberies reported by people between the ages of 12 and 19 occurred within schools. (16-17)

-Kenneth V. Hardy & Tracey A. Laszloffy, Teens Who Hurt

11 YEARS OLD

Welcome to Junior High

This was my first year of middle school and all of the kids made fun of me, as usual. They made fun of my clothes and my haircuts. My dad used to cut my hair and while everybody else was getting fades my dad was giving me bowl cuts. Many of the kids began to sell drugs so they had money to buy expensive clothing and jewelry but my clothes were far from in-style.

Middle school was different from elementary school because in elementary school you might get pushed down in the sandbox or clipped up on the soccer field; but in middle school people were getting beat down and stomped out. I was in constant fear. My school was a war zone.

Behind the Wall

During the first week of middle school, some older kids were hanging out at our bus stop when we got off the bus. Then another bus from a different school came down the hill and the dudes that were hanging out at our bus stop threw rocks at the bus. One of the girls riding on that bus got hit in the head with a rock. The kids on that bus were from a different neighborhood than we were but some of them knew me because I went to the same elementary school as they did. Since I was the only kid that they knew at our bus stop they told the bus driver that I threw the rocks.

The next day after we got off of our bus their bus came down the hill again and their bus driver followed us down into our neighborhood. The kids from the bus were cursing and spitting at us. Then the bus driver said that he was going to let the kids off of the bus so they could whup our asses for throwing rocks at them.

At this time, they were driving along side of us while we were walking home then they started yelling, "Terrence Jones we gonna fuck you up for throwing rocks at us." I immediately got scared and ran. The other boys that rode my bus ran as well and we all hid behind this elementary school wall that was in our neighborhood.

As we all hid behind the wall I could hear all of those kids on that bus screaming my name and saying that they were going to fuck me up. I was scared to death but I got tired of hearing them scream my name and blaming me for something that I didn't do so I came out from behind the wall and told them I didn't throw the rocks but if they wanted to get off the bus then get off. I didn't care anymore and I had made up my mind not to run home. I looked at the bus driver with tears in my eyes then he ended up pulling off.

When I turned around to pick up my book bag I saw that all of the other kids had come from behind the wall as well and had been standing behind me. I didn't understand how these boys who were older and bigger than I was were also afraid and hid behind the wall. These were the same boys who had been picking on me since I was five years old and now they were standing behind me.

12 YEARS OLD

In The Face

One day in the seventh grade while I was on the way back from lunch, I went to the bathroom and this older boy came in the bathroom and started picking on me. I told him to leave me alone and the next thing I know he punched me in the face. I had never been punched in the face before. My instincts took over and before I could even think about it, I hit him back and we started fighting.

This was the first time that I had ever fought somebody back and this was also the first time I had ever been suspended from school for anything. I just could not understand why everybody kept picking on me. I was getting fed up. After that fight, I said to myself, that wasn't that bad. Actually, it was kind of liberating and I felt at peace with myself for the first time in my life. I finally fought back.

Dancing Machine

I went to a house party at one of my friend's houses one weekend. Everybody knew that I was shy and when I was dancing with one girl, all of a sudden all of the other girls came and started dancing around me. I got real nervous then one of the girls started laughing and said that I couldn't dance then everybody started laughing at me. I made a vow never to dance again.

Because of this incident I didn't even go to my eighth grade prom even though there were plenty of girls who wanted me to take them. I became severely insecure and fearful of trying new things in front of a group of people, especially things that I knew I wasn't good at.

13 YEARS OLD

Where Y'all From?

At the beginning of my eighth grade year, three of my friends and I stayed after school to watch a basketball game that one of the local radio hosts was sponsoring at our school. I was supposed to call my mother to pick us up afterwards. I was unable to call her after the game because they had the section of the school closed off where the pay phones were. So my friends and I decided to walk and use one of the pay phones at the shopping center that was about a half mile from the school.

It was night time and as we were walking, these two other dudes started walking with us. I didn't know these two guys but one of my friends did. All of a sudden we looked up and it was about twenty guys behind us and they started yelling, "A, where y'all from?" Most of them were high school kids. Come to find out, one of their friends had gotten beaten up by a rival neighborhood and the two guys that were walking with us were from that neighborhood. Therefore, they concluded that we were all from that neighborhood and then they proceeded to beat the crap out of us.

We managed to get away and run to a shopping center nearby and we took refuge inside of one of the convenience stores. The cashier let me use the phone to call my mother. There was a police officer in the parking lot, which saved us, because a couple of those guys that jumped us had guns and I believe that if that police officer wouldn't have been there then they would have shot us. That was the first time that I had ever been jumped but it wasn't the last. My lip was busted and there was blood all over my coat. This type of thing was the norm in our neighborhoods.

David and Goliath

One day while we were at lunch somebody started a food fight and then everybody at our table starting throwing stuff in each other's food. This one dude, who was a lot bigger than me, threw a fork in my food and I threw it back in his food. Then all of a sudden, he got up and punched me in my face. My instincts kicked in again and before I knew it I had jumped up from the table and picked him up and slammed him to the floor. Then, I got on top of him and started punching him in his face. Eventually, one of the teachers pulled me off of him. I used to be scared of this dude because I was a lot smaller than he was but after that, we didn't have anymore problems.

The Boxer

There was a girl in my class who liked me, but this other guy liked her, so to impress her he started beefing with me. I wasn't the type to fight over girls but he kept pushing me. He had real fast hands because he boxed so he just knew that he could whup me.

After a while I got tired of him so, one day I told him to meet me in the bathroom after lunch and we started fighting. I didn't have time for all that boxing, so I picked him up and slammed him on the floor. Then I slammed his head into the toilet and busted his chin and blood spilled everywhere. That was it, the fight was over. I didn't have any more problems with him after that either.

The Dope Boy

There was a girl in our school who was a tomboy and one day while we were in the lunchroom she started hitting people. So this dude who was cool with her talked her into hitting me. At this point in my life I had become extremely volatile. When she hit me, I told her to stop because I was not in the mood for any drama. Then she punched me as hard as she could in my chest. Without even thinking, I pushed her so hard that she fell back into one of the lunch tables. One of the administrators saw me push her and took me to the office.

On my way to the office, this dude named Melvin who was very popular in the school looked at me and said that I was a punk for hitting a girl. Now rumors where that Melvin was getting a lot of money on the street hustling, which was evident by the way he dressed. He was a pretty boy and I despised niggas like him.

By this time, I had been in over five fights, suspended from school at least four times and sent to detention so many times that I lost count. I was no longer on the honor roll like I was in elementary school because I just didn't give a shit about anything or anyone. I was beginning to hate everybody.

When I got out of the office, my friends told me that Melvin was still talking about me. Some of them even advised me to leave him alone because he had an older brother who had a so-called reputation for being a killer or "G" (for gangsta). I took what they said into consideration and at the end of the day I walked up to Melvin and we had the following conversation,

> Me: "Hey, nigga, I heard you been talkin bout me, but here I am so say that shit to my face."

> Melvin: "I said that you was a punk for hitting a girl."

> Me: "Look here nigga, she hit me first, and what kept her from getting her ass whupped was the fact that she was a girl. But you, on the other hand, are not a girl so you gonna get the ass whuppin' that she was supposed to get."

> Melvin: "Man, whatever."

My friends grabbed me and told me to chill because the principal had warned me that if I got into any more fights he would kick me out of school for the rest of the school year and I would have to repeat the eighth grade. So then I told Melvin:

> "I'm not about to get kicked out of school for fighting your bitch ass but I'm gonna see you on the last day of school and as soon as you walk through the front doors I'm gonna beat the shit out of you."

Then I walked away. My friends said, "Terrence, what about his older brother?" My response, "I don't give a fuck about his brother. Fuck him and his punk ass brother." We had about two more months before the last day of school and every time I walked passed Melvin in the hallway I just mugged on him. When the last day of school came, I stood in the lobby waiting for Melvin but needless to say he never showed up and I passed to the ninth grade.

CONCLUSIONS

1. In order to survive with animals you have to become one.
2. I can only depend on myself because nobody else is going to look out for me.
3. Fighting feels good.

4. Never dance in front of anyone or go to any functions where people are dancing.
5. Never hang around people you don't know.
6. Bigger don't mean stronger.
7. Another man's reputation don't mean shit to me.

Self-Worthlessness

Our parents plant mental and emotional seeds in us—seeds that grow as we do. In some families, these are seeds of love, respect, and independence. But in many others, they are seeds of fear, obligation, or guilt. (5)

All parents are deficient from time to time... No parent can be emotionally available all the time... But there are many parents whose negative patterns of behavior are consistent and dominant in a child's life. These are the parents who do the harm. (5)

Whether adult children of toxic parents were beaten when little or left alone too much, sexually abused or treated like fools, overprotected or overburdened by guilt, they almost all suffer surprisingly similar symptoms: damaged self-esteem, leading to self-destructive behavior. In one way or another, they almost all feel worthless, unlovable, and inadequate. (6)

-Susan Forward, Ph.D., Toxic Parents

12 YEARS OLD

Picture Imperfect

Every year the students took school pictures and their parents purchased the pictures to give to their family and friends. During my seventh grade year on the day the pictures arrived my teacher passed out our pictures and when she got to my pictures she started laughing. Then she passed them to one of the students sitting up front to pass back to me and everybody saw my pictures and burst out laughing. When I finally saw my pictures, they were terrible. When I took the picture the camera man made me laugh then he snapped the picture. Those were the worst pictures I had ever taken in all the days of my life.

Normally my mother and father would give my school pictures to our family, but one day when I was looking through my parent's drawer for something I found those pictures and I realized that my pictures looked so bad that my own parents were ashamed of them. After that incident, I made a vow never to smile again, especially while taking pictures.

The Car is Fine

One day, during the winter months, I was riding with my mother in my father's company car when all of a sudden she drove over an ice patch in the middle of the road and lost control of the car and crashed into this brick building. I wasn't injured but my mother had hurt her knee. The car wasn't too bad and it was still drivable.

We were afraid to go home and tell my dad because we didn't know how he was going to react. I remember wishing that I had sustained a serious injury so that he wouldn't be as mad about my mother crashing the car, but more concerned about me.

When we got home my mom told my dad what had happened and he was upset but he didn't yell and scream at us. He didn't ask whether we were alright either. We didn't even care. We were just happy that he didn't lose his temper and go off on us.

Ma, What's Wrong?

My mother was a very beautiful woman, but she didn't think so. After I was born, her and my father didn't spend much time together. I don't recall anytime during my childhood that they went out as a couple to enjoy each other's company. My mother didn't have many friends and she spent a lot of time alone.

She was sad most of the time and she was always very critical of herself. She would say things like, "I'm ugly" or "I'm too fat". My mother was not ugly and nowhere near fat. I could never understand why she felt that way about herself. Seeing her sad made me sad. She always talked about leaving Maryland and going back to Memphis, Tennessee to live with her family because she was unhappy with her marriage and her job.

My mother and I spent a lot of time together. She always tried to get me what I wanted and she was also very protective of me, sometimes overprotective. She worried a lot and as a result my parents placed very strict curfews on me in regards to me hanging outside with my friends.

I always had to come in the house long before all of the other kids in the neighborhood went home and they all made fun of me for that. But whenever I was home, my mother felt safe and didn't have to worry. This led to me spending a lot of time in the house by myself. I internalized her pain and I became like my mother in a lot of ways. I always felt like I had to make her happy so she wouldn't be sad.

13 YEARS OLD

Science Fair Project

In my eighth grade year, we had to turn in a science fair project. Of course, no kid can complete their science fair project on their own and would have to solicit the help of their parents. I spoke to my mother and she helped me with the backboard presentation and my dad helped me with the actual experiment.

My project consisted of comparing the strength of a regular magnet to that of an electromagnet. We made an electromagnet by coiling a piece of copper wire around a piece of metal then hooking the coiled wire to a battery. The charge from the battery flowed through the coiled wire and generated an electromagnetic field around the metal which would attract anything else that was metal.

The next step was to build two wooden cranes, one to hang the regular magnet and one to hang the electromagnet. We used the cranes to lower both magnets into a cup with nails to see which one would attract the most nails.

My dad was very helpful with the project but when the time came to build the cranes he told me that I could do that part on my own. I had no idea how to build the cranes.

One day, I was in my basement with one of my friends trying to build the cranes and we couldn't figure out how to build them. I believe it was the day before my project was due so I had no choice but to go and ask my dad to help me. When I asked for his help, he started fussing at me then he went downstairs and started to build both of the cranes.

He complained and fussed at me the whole time. While my father was fussing at me, my friend just looked at me and starting shaking his head and I just began to look down at the floor because I could not understand why my father was so angry about helping me. When he finally finished he said, "Here, take these damn cranes. "

After that he went back upstairs to his room and shut his door. I didn't want him to build the cranes for me, I just wanted him to show me how to build them and I would have built them myself. After that incident, I didn't ask my father to help me with anymore school projects.

Predator

The summer before I went to high school, one of my cousins (my mother's nephew) from Tennessee stayed with us. One day, my cousin and I were in the basement watching TV when we heard my father upstairs in the living room yelling at my little brother who was only four years old at the time. Then my mother stepped in to defend my brother and told my father to ease up. Then, my father started yelling and cursing at her.

I was so embarrassed because my cousin had this look on his face like he was witnessing a horror movie. He wasn't used to being exposed to that type of drama and now for the first time in his life he was terrified.

I got so mad that I went upstairs and with a trembling voice, I told my father to stop yelling at my mother. My father looked at me and said, "Who you think you talking to?" I responded by saying, "I'm talking to you." Then he grabbed me and started choking me to the point where I couldn't breathe and I almost blacked out. He eventually let me go then he went back upstairs to his room and slammed the door.

I couldn't believe that he could snap and get so mad to the point of possibly killing his own son. That's when I began to hate my father because I felt like he hated me. I went back downstairs into the basement and started crying. My cousin was scared to death and he just sat still in one spot for the rest of the day and barely said a word. He was shell-shocked because he had no idea how dysfunctional our family was and how violent my dad could get. We were not the Cosby's.

That was the first time that I ever stood up to my dad. But, I realized that I was no match for him. I had just watched the movie "*Predator*," starring Arnold Schwarzenegger, and got the idea to hide a bunch of weapons around the house. I sharpened sticks and hid them along with some of the kitchen knives in every room of the house. I hid them under the pillows on the couch, in closets, and behind furniture. I figured if it goes down again, I will be able to get my hands on something that will even the playing field.

The next day, my father bust in my room with all of the weapons that I had hid and said, "Are these for me?" I just looked at him and said to myself, *"Well, that's it, I'm a dead man."* I didn't respond to his question.

To this day I have no idea how he found all of those weapons. He took all of the sticks and broke them over his knee and threw all of the weapons on my floor and said, "Only punks use weapons to fight somebody." Then he walked out of my room. I thought to myself, *"Yeah, but only punks beat up on people smaller than them."* I dared not say it to his face because I had concluded that my dad was crazy.

CONCLUSIONS

1. Never smile because my smile makes me look ugly.
2. Dad doesn't care about us.
3. I have to make my mother happy.
4. Don't ask dad for help. Just try to figure things out on your own.
5. One of these days my dad is going to kill me.

2ND Quarter:

The Affects of Trauma

2ND Quarter:

The Affects of Trauma

6

Hopeless High School Years

Repeated Trauma Also Called Type II post-traumatic stress disorder, occurs in children who have been abused often and for a long time. Chronic trauma is also common in children who have been reared in violent neighborhoods or war zones. Increasingly it is found in children who witness violence in the home or in their communities... Because the trauma is repeated or prolonged, the child develops a sickening anticipation and dread of another episode. After being repeatedly brutalized, children may have a confusing combination of feelings, at times angry and sad, at others fearful. Often these children appear detached and seem to have no feelings. Such emotional numbness is a hallmark of this type of trauma...

Tragically, trauma shatters the natural sense of invincibility and trust basic to normal childhood. This shakes the child's confidence about the future and can lead to limited expectations. Traumatized children often have a pessimistic view of career, marriage, having children, and even life expectancy.

-American Academy of Child and Adolescent Psychiatry,
Your Child – Childhood Trauma and Its Effects

14 YEARS OLD

Death Threat

It was the fall of 1990, my first year of high school, and I was scared to death; but I didn't show it. Most of my friends from middle school went to a different high school than I did, so I was pretty much on my own besides some of the guys who lived in my neighborhood.

In my community, the higher the level of school you attended also equated to the higher the level of violence you experienced. For instance, in elementary school you might get pushed on the

47

playground; in middle school you might get beat up in the bathroom. But, in high school, people were getting killed.

One day during the first month of high school, some older guys threatened me because they thought I had snitched on one of their friends when I didn't. Once again; I was being targeted for no reason. I had no family in this area, so I was always on my own. I had to watch my back everyday in school for a while until that situation blew over.

I had four more long years of this type of drama to look forward to. It seemed a person would be safer on the street than they were at school. Welcome to the jungle, freshman.

War Zone

One day while we were in school, we heard a gun shot. Later on, we found out that two students were paid by another student to kill someone he was beefing with. This was one of the first instances in the country where there was a shooting inside of a public school.

The news media came to the school to interview some of the students and teachers. Despite that incident, none of the students were really shocked or bothered by it. As a matter of fact, many of the students had already been carrying guns to school, so the shooting really wasn't a big deal.

When my Uncle Bo died, my father took Uncle Bo's "22" Revolver Pistol from my grandmother's house in Baltimore and put it in his closet. He didn't know it back then, but, I used to take it from his closet and carry it with me to school from time-to-time. I didn't have any bullets for it; but, I carried it anyway. I figured that if I was backed into a corner, then flashing the gun would buy me some time so I could make a getaway.

Blood Drive

In my freshman year, the Red Cross came to our school to conduct a blood drive. Only the seniors and juniors who were old enough could give blood. Several of the students received notification from the Red Cross that their blood could not be accepted because they had tested positive for HIV. The news ended up getting out because many of the students shared their test results with their friends seeking comfort but their friends ended up betraying their confidence and spreading their business throughout the school (so much for friends).

Anyway after hearing that news, I had made up my mind to stay away from girls because you just didn't know who had it and you couldn't tell by looking at people. My friends started calling me gay and said that I was scared of girls. I was shy and insecure when it came to talking to females, but I was more concerned about catching a sexually transmitted disease (STD). So I was and always have been real cautious when it comes to women.

Despite the news, most of the guys I knew where still having unprotected sex. As I got older, I slipped up a few times myself because over time sex became a painkiller for me.

You Have Fun

As I got older, I started hanging out with the older people in my neighborhood. One night, I went with them to a house party and I told them that I had to be back home by eleven o'clock and they said, "No problem."

When we walked into the party, everybody was getting high as a kite. That was the first time I saw people smoking weed. I didn't smoke, but a friend of mine gave me a beer. When I finished it, he gave me another one and after the second beer I was drunk as a skunk.

I kept asking them when were they going to take me home and they kept telling me everything was cool and it was only nine o'clock, then they would give me another beer. Every time I asked them what time it was they kept saying it was nine o'clock. I was too drunk to realize that they were lying to me.

I was so drunk that I ended up sitting on the floor next to this girl who was my age and she was just as green as I was when it came to partying and hanging out. While we were talking, I kept forgetting her name and by the time we finished talking I had asked her what her name was about ten times. What was even stranger than that was before I left to go home she still gave me her phone number and told me to call her.

When my friends finally took me home, I was nodding off in the car. When they pulled up to my house it was two in the morning and my house was lit up like a Christmas tree. My parents had called everybody they knew to find out where I was. Before I got out of the car, my friends asked me did I want to stay over one of their houses until I sobered up. I said, "No" because this way I won't feel the ass whuppin' that my father was about to give me.

When I stumbled into the house, I saw my dad washing dishes. I knew something was wrong because he never washed dishes and I just kept thinking to myself, *"What the hell is he doing washing dishes at two in the morning?"*

When he saw me, he walked over to me with soap suds running down his hands and asked, "You have fun?" Before I could respond, he punched me upside my head and I fell back against the wall. Then, my legs gave out and I fell down to the floor. He began to curse me out but I couldn't hear what he was saying, plus, I had soap suds running down my face getting into my eyes.

By this time I had another dog, a Rottweiler named Zeus, and after my father hit me, Zeus ran upstairs from the basement and growled at my father. I managed to crawl upstairs to my room and lay on my bed. After that, all I could hear was my father downstairs cursing Zeus out and beating him with a broom stick.

I started mumbling, "Leave my dog alone." Then, I passed out. The next morning, I woke up and the first thing I did was go downstairs into the basement and check on Zeus. I was trying to make sure that he didn't have a knot on his head. I was glad to find out that he didn't.

I realized I was wrong for hanging out so late so I could understand why my pops went upside my head. I was just surprised that he didn't choke me out because that was his finishing move.

15 YEARS OLD

Bad News

In my tenth grade year I received the worst news in my life; my mother was diagnosed with Breast Cancer. The day she went to the hospital to get her results from her exam, she told me to pray for her and I said, "Okay." Later on that day when my parents got back home, I stood on the steps and as my mother came in the house through the front door, she looked up at me, then, put her head down. I knew at that moment that her test results came back positive for cancer.

I ran into my room and slammed the door and started crying. I felt like the world was coming to an end. My father came into my room and told me that it was okay to cry but to try and refrain from crying in front of my mother because we had to be strong for her. I said, "Okay," but all I could picture was my mother's hair falling out like my grandmother's. My grandmother didn't live long with cancer, only about two and a half years, so I figured that my mother would not survive to see me graduate from high school.

I always thought about her dying and seeing her in a casket with her skin being two shades darker. The only thing that comforted me after that was anger. I started getting into more trouble at school. I stayed in the principal's office and my referral folder was thicker than an encyclopedia because of all the insubordinate write-ups turned in by my teachers. I just stopped caring. I was only fifteen years old but that news shattered all my hopes and dreams.

Dead Men Walking

One of the former students of my high school dropped his girlfriend off at the school one day. After she got out of the car and walked away, he pulled out a gun and shot himself in the head. Once the news spread throughout the school, some of the female students were crying but it didn't really faze any of the male students.

Hearing about the death of a fellow student wasn't anything new. On average, two-to-three people died per year, most of them males and most of the time the cause of death was a homicide. Unless it was a close friend of yours, the normal reaction is, "Oh well. That's too bad."

It had become commonplace for people to get killed so that type of news wasn't even shocking. We were like dead men walking because we were unable to feel anything. Typically, whenever a student was killed and the word was spread; the conversation went as follows:

Student 1: *"Hey, man did you hear about 'So and So'?"*

Student 2: *"Nah, what happened?"*

Student 1: *"He got killed last night."*

Student 2: *"For real?"*

Student 1: *"Yep!"*

Student 2: *"Damn, that's fucked up. Anyway, what are you doing after school cuz I'm going to see Keisha and she got a buddy that's phat to death. You trying to roll?"*

Student 1: *"Hell yeah, I'm wit it."*

16 YEARS OLD

Are You A Dumb Kid?

By the time I made it to the eleventh grade, I was sent to the office for just about everything: fighting, gambling, skipping class, disrupting class, forging teachers' signatures on hallway passes to get myself and my friends out of class, pulling the fire alarm (well, I never got caught doing that), throwing metal trash cans down the hallway, etc, etc. You name it, I did it. Despite all of the trouble that I was getting into, I was never in jeopardy of failing because I always did just enough work to pass.

One day, I got kicked out of class and was sent to the main office as usual. When I went into Dr. Sullivan's office (my administrator) he said, "Terrence, I have had numerous opportunities to expel you from school but I never did because I believed that you were a smart kid who acted dumb to fit in with the other dumb kids. But now I am starting to believe that you really are a dumb kid."

I got mad and said, "Who you calling dumb?" He replied, "You, and that is what I'm going to believe until you prove me wrong." Then he sent me back to class. He pissed me off when he said that. I thought to myself, *"Who the hell was he calling dumb?"*

What's Happening to Me?

During this time, my mom had a mastectomy and was undergoing chemotherapy. Her hair had fallen out and she had to wear wigs. She looked just like my grandmother. It was a very stressful time and all I kept thinking about was, *"When is she going to die and what am I going to do when she's gone?"*

Then something unusual started happening to me, I began to stutter. I never stuttered as a child but for some strange reason I couldn't pronounce certain words without stammering. I didn't stutter that often but when I did, people made fun of me. The more I tried not to think about it; the more I thought about it. The more I tried not to stutter the more I stuttered.

This made me even more insecure and caused me to become even angrier. It seemed like nothing was going right for me. This caused me to withdraw even further away from people and just keep to myself. Sometimes, I even sat by myself at lunch because I just didn't want to be bothered by anyone.

17 YEARS OLD

Go Ahead and Kill Me

Throughout all of the drama in high school, I still managed to make it to the twelfth grade. Unlike most of my friends I was in no danger of failing and I only needed to pass two classes to graduate: twelfth grade English and a Health class. I signed up for a couple of college prep courses but I didn't apply myself in those classes and eventually got discouraged and started acting up in class.

One day I got sent to the office and the principal called my mother. My mother normally would not tell my father when I got into trouble because she feared what he would do to me but by this time she was fed up with me and had no choice. So, she told my father. When my dad got home, we got into it about me getting into trouble in school and he began to yell and curse at me and I just couldn't take it anymore and I started yelling back.

The next thing you know we were fighting. He slammed me to the floor and started choking me. I couldn't get him off of me and when I looked into his eyes I didn't see anything, he had left the building. The only thing that I could do was say, "Kill me, just go ahead and kill me." When he heard me say that, he came back to his senses and said, "Son, Son." Before he could say anything else I ran out of the house crying.

My dad almost killed me, his own son. I felt like if my dad didn't give a shit about me then who else could I expect to care for me? No one, only my mother but as far as I knew she would be dead soon and I would be on my own.

High Profile Student

A friend of mine, named Mark got into an argument with another student, named Eric in our English class one morning. Mark and I lived in the same neighborhood but Eric lived around the corner from us.

Later that day after school let out, Mark had planned to fight Eric but Eric got wind of what was happening and didn't ride the school bus home. Eric's parents called the school and said that there were some kids who had threatened to kill their son. His parent's didn't know Mark's name so all they could tell the principal was what neighborhood Mark was from.

Upon receiving that limited information, the principal then concluded that I was the culprit because they knew that I lived in that neighborhood so he called my house and told my parent's that I could not return to school until they came to a meeting to determine why I was threatening the life of another student. I told my parents that I had nothing to do with it but they didn't believe me because my track record was terrible.

Eric told the truth at the meeting and said that I didn't have anything to do with it and that no one had actually threatened his life. After the meeting, my father was pissed off and asked the principal why did they automatically accuse me when they didn't have any evidence against me?

The principal told my father that I was a high profile student and what that means is if something bad is going on in the school that he knows nothing about and if I am anywhere in the vicinity of where the incident took place then chances are I either caused the incident or know who did. So, pulling me into the office will help him get to the bottom of the situation.

Basically, he was saying that I am one of the usual suspects. He apologized to my father for having him miss a day of work and for wrongly accusing me. But, he said that was the reputation that I had made for myself at the school because of all of the trouble I had gotten into. After that, my father looked at me like I was crazy. I didn't say anything. I just kept my mouth shut and went to class.

High School Graduation

I had finally made it through high school. On the day of my graduation, I had made up my mind to ride low and stay out of trouble. All I wanted to do was walk across the stage and receive my diploma and put high school behind me.

When I first arrived backstage at my graduation, I didn't know where I was supposed to line up so I asked a couple of the other students where I needed to go. There were also a few other students who didn't know where to line up either.

Then one of my former teachers who didn't like me very much started fussing at me and said that I was being disruptive. I told her I was trying to find my place in line and she said that she was going to have me kicked out of the graduation. We exchanged a few words then a couple of my friends pleaded with me to chill.

I was pissed because she singled me out but I managed to calm down because my mother had survived to see me walk across that stage and I didn't want to let her down. I just kept focusing on seeing her smile at me as I walked across the stage and that is what got me through. The administrators eventually told all of the kids who didn't know where to line up to just get to the back of the line then we all marched out and took our seats.

Because they sent a couple of us to the back of the line our names were not called in the correct order. After the graduation Dr. Sullivan walked up to me and shook my hand and said, "Terrence you know that half of that diploma is mine." I responded, "Yeah Doc, I know. Thanks a lot."

Many of the students had mixed emotions about graduating. About half of the students were happy because they had things lined up for themselves after high school; namely, college, the military, or a job. The other half of the students, were depressed because they didn't have a plan. Many of them could not afford college and didn't know what to do.

As for myself, my grades were not good enough for me to be accepted into an accredited university but I did register to attend the local community college. I knew that I was smart enough to make it in college but there was one thing that had been haunting me and it was getting worse and worse by the minute. That was stuttering.

By this time, I began to limit my conversations because I was too afraid to talk to people for fear of them laughing at me or thinking that I was stupid. The more I tried to overcome it, the worse it became. It was so bad that I had to master how to hide it. This fear of stuttering began to imprison me and it dictated how I interacted with people and how I viewed life in general.

CONCLUSIONS

1. There is nothing positive to look forward to at school.
2. In order to survive, I will need to carry a gun.
3. HIV is a death sentence.
4. Alcohol numbs the pain.
5. My mother will not be alive much longer so prepare to be on your own.
6. Never feel or show emotion because emotions are for the weak.
7. Maybe I am a dumb kid.
8. Keep to yourself because you can't talk right. You're stupid.
9. No one really cares about me, especially not my dad.
10. The principal is out to get me.
11. Stay away from anything that will cause you to speak publicly because you stutter.

The Dark Files

*Anger, in my opinion, is like energy. It cannot be destroyed, but it can be stored, its form can be changed, or it can be properly discharged. When we bury the anger within us and repeatedly deny its existence, I believe it accumulates in what I call the **unresolved anger fund**. The more we push down anger, the more deposits we make in our unresolved anger fund. This stockpiled anger will then express itself through sundry physical or emotional symptoms. As one researcher put it: "The inhibition or active holding back of thoughts, [and] emotions...can become manifested in disease....we believe that **the failure to confront trauma** forces the person to live with it in an unresolved manner." (31) ...People are like volcanoes. They can lay dormant for long periods, but when there is enough heat and pressure an eruption occurs. (34)*

-Dwight L. Carlson, M.D., Overcoming Hurts & Anger

If the soul is left in darkness, sins will be committed. The guilty one is not he who commits the sin, but he who causes the darkness.

-Victor Hugo

18 YEARS OLD

Security, Security, Man Down!

In the summer of 1995, I met a few friends of mine at one of the high end malls in Virginia. It was a total of five of us; three young black males and two young black females.

While we were at the mall, we decided to get something to eat at the food court. I was the last person to purchase my food and to sit down at the table and eat with everyone else. One of the janitors who worked in the mall was mopping the floor next to where we were eating and his walkie-talkie radio was blasting in our ears, so my friend asked him could he turn down the volume. The man said no and he and my friend began to argue with each other. Then, the janitor called for security.

When the security guard came to the table, my friend started making jokes. Then, the security guard asked us to leave the mall. I told the security guard that I had just purchased my food and hadn't had an opportunity to finish eating so he told us that we could stay until I finished eating my food, but once I finished eating to leave the mall. I said cool. In the interim he called for back up and within two minutes there were at least five other security guards standing around our table ready to escort us out of the mall.

The head security guard arrived on the scene and spoke with the security guard who told us to leave the mall and after they finished talking he walked up behind me since I was the only one still eating and kicked my chair. He kicked my chair so hard that I almost fell to the floor. Then I stood up with a mouth full of food and asked him why did he kick my chair then he pushed me in my chest. Once he pushed me, I retaliated and I began to punch, kick, knee, elbow and head-butt him.

I was so angry I couldn't even feel the other security guards hitting me. I had tunnel vision and all of my focus was on him. By the time they pulled me off of him, he was bloody from this huge gash that was over his eye.

When they stood me up, he also got up off of the floor and looked me in my eye and said that he will see me again. Then, I spit the food I had in my mouth in his face and starting cursing him out. They handcuffed me and took me to their holding station until the police came to get me.

My shirt was ripped and there was blood all over it, his blood. I overheard some of the security guards talking and they couldn't understand how someone my age and size could barely be detained by grown men. At that time, I was about 5'-10" tall and weighed about 145 lbs. The security guard who assaulted me was about 5'-11" tall and weighed about 230 lbs.

When the police officer came to escort me to her police car she walked me through the entire mall and everybody was staring at me, but I refused to put my head down and I looked everybody in their eyes as I walked past them. She could have parked in the rear of the mall and taken me out of the back door but I guess she wanted to put me on display.

I got locked up for the very first time in my life. I had been arrested before for shoplifting but never physically taken to a prison and sent to my own cell. They don't play around in Virginia. I was charged with assault and disturbing the peace.

When they took me before the magistrate, I tried to explain to him that the security guard attacked me first and I just defended myself but once he looked at the pictures and saw all the blood on that white man's face he set my bail. Then he told them to take me to a cell. I was scared to death in jail, but I was even more scared of my father coming to get me.

When I called home to tell my parents what happened my mother went off and hung up the phone. By that time she was fed up with me. I tried to explain to her that it really wasn't my fault this time but she wasn't trying to hear it.

When my father arrived at the jail, one of the police officers brought me into a room to speak to him. The police officer told me that I could approach the window and speak to my dad and I asked the officer could he break through the glass. The officer started laughing because he thought that I was playing, but I wasn't. I was serious as hell.

My father had this look on his face like he was going to punch through that glass and rip my head off. When I approached the glass, I stood about two feet away and my father asked me what happened and I told him that it didn't matter what I said because he wasn't going to believe me. I finally told him what happened and he said that he was going to get me out of there.

Later on that night, my parents came up to the jail to bail me out. It was around one in the morning. My aunts wired some money from Tennessee to help my parents post my bond. From that moment on, I stayed the hell out of Virginia.

They Shootin'

One night, a friend of mine called me, while at his girlfriend's high school prom. He told me that his ex-girlfriend's brothers, who he had been beefing with, were at the school threatening him. I didn't have a car at the time so I told him to come and pick me up so that we could handle it.

When we arrived at the school, one of our friends met us there, and we all ended up fighting. Shortly after, someone called the police, so my friend pulled me off of the dude I was fighting and we got into the car and left. We had beaten the hell out of two of them and the other one ran.

Later on that night, while my friends and I were outside of my house talking, the dudes we had just fought rode down my street and started shooting at us. Several bullets hit my house and one even went through my little brother's bedroom window. My mother and father woke up and began to panic. Nobody got shot and when the police finally arrived, they filed a report.

I had vowed to kill them but the police ended up locking one of them up before I could find him. The other guy left town to stay with his father. Before he got locked up, I was looking for him. I even spent the night in my car outside of his apartment building waiting for him to come home but I never caught up with him.

The same friend who I was fighting for was too scared to ride with me when it was time to retaliate. I was hurt because I only got involved because he called me to help him, but now he wouldn't even help me. I cut him off after that and never kicked it with him again. Up until that point, I had considered him as one of my closest friends and I was so hurt that I even cried. I thought that he was my man, but I was wrong.

19 YEARS OLD

You're Fired!

I managed to get my first job loading trucks in the warehouse at this big-time delivery company. Three of my friends and I applied for the company, but only two of us got hired. The work was strenuous and my friend ended up hurting his back, so he eventually quit but I stayed on because I needed the extra money for college expenses.

I managed to work there for a year and a half. I was one of the best loaders there and was even offered a position to become a trainer, but I turned it down because I had no plans of making a career out of it.

The warehouse was divided into belts and each belt had about ten bays where the company drivers would dock their trailers for loading. Our belt was so good, that we didn't even need a supervisor.

Eventually, they were transitioning one of the supervisors who worked in the small sorting department to work downstairs in the warehouse, so they assigned him to our belt because it would be easier for him to oversee our belt versus one of the other belts.

He never knew what he was doing and everyday he would get the orders wrong and jam up our belt. We were all getting pissed off with him because the more jams that we got on the belt the longer we had to stay at work.

From time-to-time, the supervisors would test the loaders to make sure that they were not loading the wrong packages on the trucks. They would put a package with an incorrect zip code (miss-sort) on your truck without you knowing it to see if you would load it.

One day while we were extremely busy, he put a miss-sort on my truck and I caught it. Then, I walked outside of the truck and asked him why doesn't he come in the trucks and help us load the boxes instead of standing outside putting miss-sorts on the truck.

All of the other supervisors would get in the trucks and help the workers load their trucks when the belts got backed up. However, he seemed to be more concerned about writing people up rather than getting the trucks loaded on time.

We argued for a while and afterwards I went back into my truck and kept working. After that, every time I caught a miss-sort, I would throw it out of my truck.

One day, he sent one of the guys in the truck to work with me who was on the verge of getting fired because he wasn't doing well. He had just gotten out of jail and was trying to stay out of the drug game, so I had sympathy for him.

As we were loading my truck, I heard the supervisor yell "Miss-sort" then he came in my truck and pulled the miss-sort from the boxes we loaded. The supervisor looked at him and said that he was terminated because he had already been warned about loading miss-sorts.

I told the supervisor that I did it (because he didn't actually see who loaded the miss-sort) and he said no I didn't. I told him again, that I loaded the miss-sort, so he said, "Fine," and that he was going to put it on my record. I told him to stop wasting our time and get his ass out of the truck and go put it on my record. I just could not understand why he was so intent on getting people fired. He was really and I mean really pissing me off.

The next day, I came to work he told me that he was reassigning me to another belt and the belt he was sending me to was the worst belt in the warehouse. I told him I wasn't going and he told me that if I didn't go, he was going to have me terminated.

Before I knew it, we were arguing and I began to curse him out and a couple of my coworkers tried to calm me down. He told me that he was going to have me fired for insubordination and for threatening him. We had to go to the head supervisor's office and he told them that I threatened his life and that I had been a disruption on the belt. He also said that I had been loading miss-sorts and that I was incompetent.

He was lying like hell. The only miss-sort that was on my record was the one that I took for my friend. I barely even talked to anyone on the belt because I kept to myself and the average person loaded about one and a half trucks a day and my average was three trucks a day. The more he lied, the angrier I got and I just couldn't control myself. After hearing what he said they fired me on the spot. I was so mad, I felt like choking him out. Sounds familiar doesn't it.

One of the union representatives came to my defense and tried to calm me down, but couldn't. He was an older guy and he said, "Young man calm down. Go home and cool off and in a couple of days they will call you in for a review and I already spoke with them and since you are such a good worker they will give you your job back if you apologize."

I went home but I was upset and ashamed because that was my first job and I had been fired. That was his plan all along; to fire me and like a dummy, I took the bait. I was so upset that I had visions of killing him. I seriously thought about catching him going to his car one evening after work and beating him down. The only reason I didn't was I knew they would have known that it was me and I wasn't trying to go back to jail again.

When the union representative called my house and told me my appeal date, I told him to tell them that they can take that job and stick it up their asses because I wasn't going to bow down and apologize to nobody. He asked me if I was sure and I said yeah. Then he said, "Okay, young man," and then I hung up.

Road Rage

One night after I left one of the local clubs, this car ran into the back of me and smashed my trunk in. The guy took off before I could get his information and I was left with a banged up car.

I rode around looking for him and couldn't find him, so I pulled up on these police officers to ask for their assistance. When I walked up to one of the officers to ask him if he could file a police report because somebody had crashed into my car and fled the scene, he began to curse me out and told me to get back into my car because they were busy. I just got in my car and left after that.

My friend warned me not to open the trunk but I had to get something out of it and when I did, I couldn't get it closed again. So, I had to tie my trunk down with a piece of rope. When I got home, my father fussed at me about the car and said that we didn't have the money to get it fixed so I had to ride around with my trunk flapping.

One day while I was out driving, I looked in my rear view mirror and I saw these two older guys in their car behind me laughing. I realized that they were laughing at my car, so I pulled over in the next lane and let them pull up alongside of me and I asked them what they were laughing at. Then one of them threw his drink on my car and they both started laughing again.

I sat there and thought for a minute and said to myself, *"What the hell. My car is already fucked up,"* so I rammed into the side of their car. They started screaming and I kept ramming them. I said, "Yeah nigga, ya'll ain't laughing now. Your car looks worse than mine, you bitch ass niggas!" Then they pulled over and I kept driving.

Later on, I couldn't believe what I had done. However, this was my m. o. (modus operandi). Whenever I became angry, I just snapped and by the time I came back to my senses there would be no telling what I had done. I was similar to Bruce Banner after he had changed back from being the Incredible Hulk, awakening to find out that he had left a trail of total destruction.

Look At His Face

Me and a friend of mine were hanging out at one of the clubs one night where a local Go-Go band was performing. When I turned around and looked, I saw one of the guys who had shot at my house standing right behind me. He didn't even realize that I was standing in front of him because the club was packed. I told my friend about him and we left to go to my house so I could get my shotgun.

Two of my other friends met us back at the club and we sat in our cars and waited for him to come out. As the club let out, I saw a car pull off that looked like his car so we followed it. When the car finally stopped at this house I got out of my car and ran up to the dude and put my shotgun to his head. Right before I pulled the trigger I heard a voice say, *"Look at his face."* When the man turned around, I realized it was the wrong guy. I immediately turned around and ran back to my car. My friends asked me what happened and I told them it wasn't him and that I almost killed somebody for nothing.

20 to 21 YEARS OLD

Self-Destruction

During this time in my life, I had been getting into all types of trouble. I was stealing, fighting, drinking, fornicating, shooting guns, etc. This was a very dark time in my life and I had absolutely no compassion for anyone.

I treated women terribly and had absolutely no respect for them. My relationships with women never lasted over three months because I was incapable of acquiring feelings for them because I didn't have any feelings. I didn't even love myself, so there was no way I was going to be able to love anyone else.

Whenever I went out to a club or social event, I ended up getting kicked out or getting into a physical confrontation with someone. On several occasions, I drank so much that I passed out. I had so much internal strife that I couldn't even go out and have fun unless I had some alcohol in my system.

I was mad at the world, especially God. My grandmother always told me that God was all powerful and that He was in control of everything. Therefore, I felt that if He was in control of everything then He was to blame for all of the bad things I was experiencing.

One day I was hanging on the corner with my friends and a couple of street ministers, who were in their late twenties, approached us. They started testifying to us about the goodness of God and His plan for salvation.

Most of my friends walked away but I stayed and I began to debate with them defiantly about God's goodness. I became so hostile that the street ministers walked away and said that they would pray for me. I told them that I didn't need their prayers. For all intents and purposes, I ran them off the block.

However, despite all of the trouble I was getting into, I still managed to pass all of my classes at the local community college. I even made the Dean's list one semester. My parent's just could not understand how someone so intelligent could get involved in some of the dumbest situations.

My mother's cancer had gone into remission for a couple of years, but during this time it came back even worse. While my mother was struggling to fight cancer, I was running the streets getting into trouble.

I was selfish and I didn't care about anyone but myself. I had become a monster. That was the time when my mother looked at me one day and said, "Terrence you have become just like your Uncle Lawrence."

CONCLUSIONS

1. Black people don't stand a chance in the judicial system.
2. Real friends don't abandon you.
3. All white people stick together and you have to learn how to play their game.
4. Don't ever let anyone disrespect you.
5. Don't ignore your inner voice.
6. Nobody cares about me, so why should I care about anyone else.
7. God is not good. If He is good then why does He allow so much bad stuff to happen?

8

Pain

Your pain is the breaking of the shell that encloses your understanding.

-Kahlil Gibran

There is no coming to consciousness without pain.

-Carl Gustav Jung

20 Years Old

University of Maryland at College Park

I spent two years at the local community college and in that time I had developed my study habits and managed to maintain a 3.5 GPA. As a result of my 180 degree turn in my studies I got accepted into the University of Maryland at College Park Clark School of Engineering Program.

At that time UMCP's engineering program was ranked in the Top Ten among all of the engineering programs across the nation. This meant that I had to step up my game and cut back on running the streets with my friends.

I was able to hide the fact that I stuttered at the community college because the work was not as difficult and I did most of my work on my own. However, at UMCP, the work was horrendous and many of the projects that you are assigned require you to work in groups.

In addition to that, UMCP is a predominately white school. I had never been around so many white people in my life. This caused me to feel even more insecure and caused my stuttering to intensify. I was constantly stressed and focused on stuttering. I felt like a disgrace to my race because whenever I stuttered in front of the white students, I felt like it validated some of their assumptions that black people are ignorant.

As a result, I began to hate myself. I would never raise my hand in class to ask a question, but I would hold all of my questions until the end of class and talk to the professor in private. I was in constant fear and as a result I kept to myself.

The pain of stuttering became unbearable and sometimes I felt like killing myself. I could not get control over it. What made it worse was that I could not figure out for the life of me how it began in the first place. All I could do was master how to hide it. But the more I hid it, the more I died on the inside.

One Handed Bandit

By this time my mother's second breast had been removed. The cancer began to spread and take a toll on her physically. Up until this point, she never physically looked sick but now she starting to lose weight. The radiation treatments had burned her skin in several areas causing her skin color over her entire body to become two-toned. But that's not all.

One day, she had surgery because the doctors had to remove some lymph nodes from her neck and they accidentally cut some nerves that controlled her arm and hand. They told her that as a result of the nerve damage, she would have limited use of her hand. For years after the surgery, my mother had to constantly shake her arm and ball her hand into a fist to help the blood circulate in her hand to keep it from going numb.

The more she suffered, the worse I felt. There was nothing we could do for her. I tried to stay positive, but it was hard. Despite all that she was going through, she continued to go to church and keep the house clean. She loved to keep us fed and on Thanksgiving she didn't miss a beat. That year, Thanksgiving dinner was so good that one of my father's friends nicknamed her, the *"One Handed Bandit."*

Give God A Shot

Every once in a blue moon I would go to church with my mother and my younger brother. One Sunday morning, when I woke up to get ready to go to church, I saw that my father had one of his suits on. I asked my mother what funeral was he going to and she said that he wasn't going to a funeral. Then I asked her what wedding was he going to and she said that he wasn't going to a wedding. Finally I asked, "Well, where else could he be going?" She said he was going to church with us. I said to myself, *"Hell no, to church, my father, going to church. Is he dying or something?"*

I responded this way because the only time I saw my father in a church was at a funeral or a wedding. When we got to church, I wasn't paying any attention to the Pastor's sermon. I just kept staring at my father, trying to figure out what he was up to.

He went to church again the following Sunday. When the Pastor finished his sermon and asked if anyone would like to come down and give their life to Christ, my father stood up and walked down the aisle. I couldn't believe it! Next thing I know, my little brother (who was twelve years old at the time) walked down the aisle behind him. My mother started crying and I even shed a tear myself. My father and my brother both got saved on the same day.

When my father gave his life to Christ, he really began to change. Some time later, I overheard him talking to one of his friends who was still running the streets. His friend asked what led him to get saved. My father told him that he was ready to throw in the towel and abandon his family because of the pain he was experiencing from his wife suffering from cancer and his son (me) getting into trouble. He said that after searching his heart, he had made up his mind that before he would abandon his family, he would first give God a shot.

21 YEARS OLD

Prisoners of the State

Although my friends and I cut up and got into a lot of trouble together, hanging out with them was the only fun that I really had. Running the streets with them helped to alleviate much of the anxiety that I was dealing with. I was severely stressed due to the relentless UMCP engineering program, my mother suffering from cancer, my father and I bumping heads, and my stuttering problem.

However, hanging out together came to an end when two of my closest friends, Kevin and Andre, got locked up. Andre was a couple of years younger than I was and his older brother had just been killed a couple of months prior. I was no substitute for his brother, but I tried to look out for him as best I could.

My other friend, Kevin, was a couple of years older than I was. Kevin was the only person that really looked out for me. We met when I was sixteen years old. I do have older brothers and sisters from my father's previous marriage, but I didn't grow up with them. So there was nobody that I looked to for help or support. However, when I met Kevin he took me under his wing and taught me a lot of things regarding the street. Even though some of the things that he taught me were wrong, it didn't matter to me because at least he took the time to teach me something.

Despite his involvement in the drug game, he still had a good heart. When I got fired from my first job, I went to him and asked him to "put me on" (give me some drugs to sell). I had never sold drugs before, but I was desperate for some money. He looked at me like I was crazy then he just walked away. I grabbed him and asked him again and he said, "Hell no!"

I got pissed off and asked him why not, because he had most of our other friends hustling for him. He told me that they didn't aspire for anything beyond the streets, but I was different. He said that I needed to focus on getting my engineering degree and starting my own business one day. Then come back and rescue guys like him. But in the mean time, if I needed some money he would give it to me. Otherwise, if he caught me out on the strip hustling, he would whup my ass and whup the person's ass who gave me the drugs to sell. Then he walked away.

Hey, that's Kevin, he's a real dude. He always had my best interest in mind even when I didn't. When he got locked up, I was heartbroken. I cried because I finally had a real friend and now he was gone and I was back on my own again.

What, You Leaving Me?

When I was twenty years old, I met this girl who really captured my attention because there was something different about her. Unlike the other girls that I met during that time, she wasn't running the streets and she wasn't involved with a lot of men. She had an innocence about herself that drew me to her and I realized that she was somebody I could trust.

Our relationship started off pretty good. I used to spend a lot of time at her house. I was even tight with her mother. But over time, I started tripping. Whenever she did something that I didn't like, no matter how insignificant, I would go off. I would call her names and curse her out over dumb stuff.

Whenever I was stressed (which was most of the time) I would take it out on her. Every now and then she would get fed up with me but then I would apologize and we would make up. However, the reconciliation would be short lived and I would turn around and be right back to fussing at her again.

I ruined her birthday and followed up by not buying her anything for Valentine's Day (not knowing that she had bought gifts for me). My response was, "My bad." It was funny to me.

I don't know why, but I just couldn't be nice to her no matter how hard I tried. I took her through hell and back and she spent many days and nights stressing over me.

Then it happened, Aretha Franklin released her song, *"A Rose is a Rose"* and Lauryn Hill released *"Ex-Factor."* After hearing those two songs she had been empowered and I was dethroned. She said that she wanted out of the relationship and I couldn't believe it. My response was, "What, you leaving me? Don't nobody leave me. I leave them." She said, "Well, whatever, but I don't want to be with you anymore." Then she was gone.

I was crushed. I had never felt any pain like that in all the days of my life. I didn't realize how much I really cared about her until it was over. I felt like Prince, "I hate you but I love you, but I can't love you, because I hate you."

One day when I was sitting on my bed, I felt something fall on my hand. When I looked up I realized that it was a tear. I said to myself, *"Oh shit! I'm crying."*

I Surrender

When my father got saved, I didn't know if he was really going to switch up, but he did. He didn't fuss with me as much and he was more attentive and supportive of my mother. He really was a changed man. After I saw his transformation, I prayed to God and asked God to remove those things in my life that were hindering me from giving my life to Him.

I was raised to believe in God, but I had strayed far away from Him and I realized that I needed to get myself together. At this point in my life, I was under a lot of stress and I needed a way out and nothing else I tried was working. So, I decided to give God a shot. This is when I learned, be careful what you pray for because you just might get it. When I prayed that prayer, I expected God to take away my anger, lust, and things of that nature. But, He had something different in mind.

One day I woke up in the middle of the night in a lot of pain. I was suffering due to seeing my mother sick with cancer, my friends getting locked up, the grueling UMCP engineering program, stuttering, and having my heartbroken by my ex-girlfriend. I began to pray and ask God what was going on and why was He allowing me to experience so much pain? Then I heard an internal voice that said,

> *"This is what you asked Me for. I have removed those things from your life that you honored above Me and I have allowed this pain to bring you to your knees. The only way you are going to survive is if you surrender to Me."*

The next Sunday, I went to church and walked down the aisle like my father did a couple of months prior and gave my life to Christ. God you win.

CONCLUSIONS

1. I am an embarrassment to my race.
2. Cancer treatments are worse than cancer itself.
3. Dad done got saved! There is a God.
4. My friends are gone. I'm on my own again.
5. Relationships don't work so don't let your guards down again.
6. I need to give God a shot like my pops did.

9

The Shadow of Death

*No person experiences an emotion just in his "heart" or in his "mind." Rather, a person experiences an emotion in the form of chemical reactions in the **body** and the **brain**. These chemical reactions occur at both the organ level—stomach, heart, large muscles, and so forth—and at the **cellular** level. (9) ...The emotions that are most damaging are rage, unforgiveness, depression, anger, worry, frustration, fear, grief, and guilt. (20)...Some fears occur repeatedly in the same environment...In these cases, the fear is called a phobia. (98)... Part of the definition of a phobia is that it is a crippling fear. It keeps a person from moving about normally in society. (99)*

-Don Colbert, M.D., Deadly Emotions

*In the most general sense, stuttering is defined as a **disruption in the flow of speech**. This disruption is often evident to the listener and the speaker...**Psychogenic stuttering** is more difficult to define and diagnose, but is understood to include stuttering resulting from psychological trauma and stuttering that is associated with mental health issues*

-The Veils of Stuttering

22 YEARS OLD

Physics Tutorial Class

The engineering course work was so hard at UMCP that it was impossible to pass your classes unless you took advantage of the teacher's assistant hours outside of class. One day, I went to one of the physics tutorial classes to get some help with my homework and there were about nine other people there; as well, who were all getting help with the same homework assignment.

While the teacher's assistant was going over one of the homework problems, I decided to brave the waters and raise my hand to ask a question. When he called on me, I couldn't get a particular word out and I stuttered terribly. I was the only black person in the class at that time and while I was struggling to say the word one of the white students said, "What he's trying to say is," then he said the word and everybody starting laughing.

I was humiliated and became very angry, which then turned into depression. I began to feel even more inferior to the white students. It was very painful and the fear of stuttering was constantly looming over me. I dreaded having to talk to people.

Library Front Desk

I got a job at the undergraduate library on campus and for the most part I was responsible for re-shelving books and repairing books that had been damaged. Eventually they promoted me and trained me to work at the front desk. I had never worked a customer service job before and I was terrified.

On one particular occasion, a woman came to the counter to return some books and she was extremely rude because she didn't want to pay her late fees. The more I tried to explain to her the late fee policy and how much she owed, the more irate she became. Then I stuttered on a couple of words and she began to laugh and make fun of me. She asked if I could get somebody to help her who could talk properly. Then I got angry and told her that regardless of who she spoke with, she will have to pay the late fees.

The more incidents like this that occurred, the more I died on the inside. There was no escape. I even made up my mind not to have kids because I felt like I would pass this curse on to them. It would break my heart to see my kids stuttering. I was in hell.

23 YEARS OLD

Suicidal Interview

I was in my last year of college and began to go on job interviews. On one of my first interviews, I was extremely nervous and I stuttered on just about every word I said. Even during the interview, the man who was interviewing me told me to relax.

At the end of the interview, the guy told me that I wouldn't be a good fit for their company. That really rocked me because I realized that stuttering was robbing me of my future.

This was the time where I seriously began to contemplate suicide. I had no hope. I tried to share with people about my inability to talk without stuttering, but nobody understood. I even went to a speech therapist, but that didn't help. People prayed for me, especially my mother, but I didn't get any better.

I even met with my pastor and he told me that stuttering was a thorn that God had given to me and I just had to learn to live with it. I didn't want to live with it. Why would God want me to live with something that was destroying my soul? I had reached a point where I believed that the only solution that was left for me was to kill myself.

One of the only reasons I didn't kill myself was I couldn't figure out how to do it so it wouldn't look like I committed suicide. I wanted to spare my family the shame of me not being able to cope with the hardships of life by killing myself. So, I worked harder at mastering how to hide stuttering by avoiding words I knew I would stutter on if I tried to say them.

I had built a prison for myself. I avoided all social gatherings where I would have to interact with people and I just kept to myself because stuttering followed me everywhere. It became my shadow.

CONCLUSIONS

1. Avoid all public speaking events.
2. Don't have kids because you are going to curse them.
3. You can't conquer stuttering so hide it.

10

Adversity

Stewart Emery reports a startling experiment done with amoebas in California. In his book "Actualizations", he reveals how two tanks of amoeba were set up in order to study the conditions most conductive to growing living organisms... In one tank, the amoebas were given ultimate comfort. The temperature, humidity, water levels, and other conditions were constantly adjusted for ultimate ease in living and proliferation. In the other tank, the amoebas were subjected to rude shocks. They were given rapidly whipsawing changes in fluid level, temperature levels, protein, and every other condition they could think of...To the total amazement of the researchers, the amoebas in the more difficult conditions grew faster and stronger than those in the comfort zone. They concluded that having things too set and too perfect can cause living things to decay and die, whereas adversity and challenge lead to strength and the building of the life force. (60)

-Steve Chandler, Reinventing Yourself

23 YEARS OLD

Ego Maniac Computer Tech

The undergraduate library was in the transition of closing down and the student workers were being let go so to supplement my income I had applied to be a computer technician at the graduate library. I did well on the interview and I was hired as well as two other people, a white male and a white female student.

We had two supervisors, a graduate student named Usef and the senior supervisor, a black man named Egor. This was the job I had been praying for. I finally had an opportunity to work for black people. I wasn't expecting any handouts only a fair shake and a chance for quality training and advancement because in case engineering didn't work out I had planned to pursue a career in the information technology field. As I said earlier, be careful what you pray for because you just might get it.

Usef was cool and took the time to really train and coach the new employees but Egor was arrogant and spoke to everyone like they were ignorant and incompetent. Everyday he would say something purposeful to destroy your self-worth. He bullied his employees but would suck up to his white male superiors and the white women who worked in the office.

He would send me on the hardest jobs knowing that I was inexperienced just so he could talk about how incompetent I was. However, he would send the white female student on jobs that were simple and praise her continuously in front of everybody.

I could not figure this man out to save my life. How could somebody be so heartless and cruel to people who hadn't done anything to him. It was as if he got joy and satisfaction out of making your life miserable. He made that job a living hell for his employees, especially the men.

I only worked there for two months then I had to resign because the stress of working for Egor began to affect my school work. I only had one semester left of school and I wasn't going to risk failing a class and lowering my GPA to continue to work for him.

Sahid

I met a very intelligent young man named Sahid, who had graduated from Howard University and received his Bachelor of Science Degree in Civil Engineering. He had enrolled in UMCP's Engineering Graduate Program and one of the classes that he had to take was an engineering course that had a mixture of graduate students and undergraduate students.

Sahid and I were the only two black men in the class, so we formed a study group along with and Indian student named, Jamal. One day while we were studying, Sahid picked up my Bible that I had on the table and began to flip through it. I got excited because I figured that this was my opportunity to share the gospel with him, but I didn't realize it was a set up.

I asked him had he read the Bible and he said plenty of times. I then asked him if he was a Christian and he said no, he was Muslim. He said that his dad was a Baptist preacher but could never answer the questions he had regarding Christianity and after studying several religions, Islam made the most sense, so he converted.

From that point on, Sahid began to explain to me the reason why he converted to Islam was due to all of the inconsistencies he found in the Bible. He even brought a paper to class the next day that he wrote. The title was *"Islam versus Christianity."*

After I read that paper, I was so confused that I didn't know what to believe. I went and spoke to my father hoping that he could help me reaffirm my faith in the Bible, but he began to fuss at me and say that I should be grounded in what I believe and not let someone confuse me. I was so pissed off with him that I left.

Then, I went and spoke with my pastor and he began to give me some religious mumbo-jumbo that didn't make any sense. The more I spoke with people trying to get some answers to help me combat Sahid's paper, the more confused I became.

One day, as I walked across the school parking lot to my car, I began to cry and I prayed and asked God to help me decide what I needed to do because I just wanted to know the truth. Then I heard a voice that said, "Before you make any decisions, first read and study for yourself."

After that, I went and bought a Study Bible and downloaded several Bible commentaries and began to study. It was a very challenging time because, while I was studying trying to determine which religion to follow, my father was pissed off with me about my confusion and Sahid kept hounding me every time he saw me about converting.

First Engineering Job

During my last semester of college, I applied and was hired part-time at a Civil Engineering firm that was located in the same area as UMCP. My schedule was pretty hectic but I was extremely motivated because I knew that if I did well at this job, they would hire me as a full-time employee once I graduated.

The work wasn't difficult, but it also wasn't what I really wanted to do. I wanted to be a Structural Engineer, but this was a Civil Engineering firm so I continued to look and apply for Structural Engineering positions.

About two weeks before I graduated, my supervisor met with me and presented me with an offer to come on-board full-time. He only offered me $33,000 even though at that time the entry level salary for engineers, especially engineers with a degree from a school like UMCP, was $36,000.

A Filipino friend of mine graduated a semester before me and worked for this same company and they offered him $37,000, but he took a job at another firm for more money. I couldn't believe that they were only offering me $33,000. I asked him why he made me such a low offer and asked if it was because of my performance and he said it wasn't. He also said that I was a great worker but $33,000 was all the company could afford to pay me at that time. I told him that I would get back with him regarding my decision.

One day, I received an email from a Structural Engineering firm informing me that they had an opening and wanted me to come in for an interview. I went to the interview and was hired on the spot. They only offered me $35,000 but I took it because it was what I really wanted to do and it was $2,000 more than what the Civil Engineering firm offered me.

When I went back and gave my supervisor my two weeks notice, he was disappointed and didn't want me to leave. He asked me if it was because of the money. He told me if it was then he would increase the original offer that he made me. I told him my decision was not based solely on the money, but because I was more interested in Structural Engineering.

Once I left his office, I asked myself, how could he all of a sudden come up with more money to pay me? I guess he figured that I was desperate and that I wouldn't be able to find an engineering job somewhere else. But, I also knew that if I was white, he would have paid me what I was worth.

College Graduation

I sent out several invitations for my college graduation, but only a handful of people showed up. I was disappointed, but at the same time, I was overjoyed because as I looked out across that auditorium I saw my mother sitting in the audience. She was still alive! This is the moment that she had prayed for, which was for God to allow her to live to see me graduate from college.

Her condition was worsening and she didn't have much strength, but she put on her favorite wig and was sitting in that auditorium smiling from ear-to-ear.

Every semester, I sat at the dining room table studying those engineering books feeling overwhelmed and I would say to my mother, "Ma, this is too hard. I can't do this. I'm not going to make it through this program," but every time I said something like that she would respond, "You said that last semester, but you made it then, and you'll make it now." Whenever she made that statement, I would shut up and keep studying.

She inspired me. If she could struggle to survive by battling cancer, then surely I could struggle to conquer that engineering program. Dr. Sullivan got me through high school, but my mother got me through college.

Glass Ceiling Profession

After graduation, I immediately began to work at the Structural Engineering firm. I was the youngest engineer that worked for the company and at that time I was the only black engineer that worked there, as well. I felt like I had to represent, so I made it my goal to break whatever stereotypes that they may have held against black people: I was never late to work, I was the first person in the office, I never took lunch breaks over the time allotted, I met all of my deadlines, and I never called out slick (I mean sick).

The reason why I bust my butt like I did was during my interview I asked for more than $35,000 per year but my supervisor told me that was all he could afford to pay me at the time, but if I worked hard and proved myself in six months after I had my first review, he would increase my salary to reflect my contribution to the company. So I took him at his word and set out to prove myself.

When it was time for my six month review, I met with my supervisor and he handed me a copy of the evaluation that he conducted regarding my work performance. There were over ten categories that I was evaluated on and I didn't receive anything lower than 85%. As a matter of fact, I scored 90% and above in most of the categories. After reviewing my evaluation, I felt pretty confident that he would increase my salary to reflect what was customary for engineers in my position.

But to my surprise, he didn't and he threw me a curve ball. He said that he still couldn't pay me what I wanted and that I needed to pass the Engineering-In-Training (E.I.T.) Exam and sign up to become a member of various Engineering Societies. Once I passed the exam and was accepted into a few of the Engineering Societies he would then increase my salary to what I wanted at my yearly review.

So, I signed up and took a review course to prepare for the E.I.T. exam. I also signed up to become a member of several Engineering Societies with hopes that once I passed the exam and my memberships were established, I would be sure to receive fair compensation for my hard work.

After six months of collecting engineering magazines that I didn't read from these Engineering Societies and after passing my E.I.T. exam, I was ready for my yearly review.

When my yearly review came up, I handed him my E.I.T. certificate and yet again he threw me another curve ball. He said that it was good that I passed the E.I.T. exam and was affiliated with several Engineering Societies, but he still couldn't pay me what I wanted because I needed to pass the Professional Engineering (P.E.) Exam.

I responded by saying, that you can only take the P.E. exam when you have four years of experience, so you're saying that I will have to wait three more years to be justly compensated. He said sorry, but that was their policy but not to worry because he knew that I would pass the exam. That's when I realized that he was never going to pay me what I was worth.

One day, I rode with him to meet with this architectural firm to discuss a project that we were working on. On the way back to the office we were talking and he told me something that at the time, I couldn't figure out if it was something that he slipped up and said or if it was something that he meant to say on purpose. He told me that before they hired me, they actually hired a white student from another college but he bailed out on them at the last minute and accepted an offer to work for a bigger firm. So, they ended up hiring me instead because he had to fill the position.

My supervisor and I had bumped heads on a few occasions, so I figured that statement he made was calculated. That's when I realized that there wasn't a future for me at that company because I was black and they would rather have a white man working for them instead of me. I immediately started looking for another job.

To be honest, this was no big surprise because when they sent me out on my first inspection and I turned in my inspection report, two of my supervisors kept saying how impressed they were with my writing abilities. They thought that they were giving me a compliment and didn't realize that this was an insult. I thought to myself, *"I graduated from one of the top schools in the nation so why are you so surprised with my ability to articulate myself in a report?"* I couldn't believe it.

Not too long after that I found another structural engineering job and gave them my two weeks notice. I had worked for that company for over two and a half years. This new firm was much larger and they paid me more money but in the end, I faced the same challenges as the previous firm and realized that there was no real opportunity for advancement.

During this time I made up my mind to seek my own career in real estate development and set out to be my own boss. So, I signed up and took several real estate classes and eventually got my real estate license.

At the age of twenty-seven, I resigned from the field of engineering. I was very disappointed because I spent six long years working my butt off in college to get my engineering degree only to realize that it was a glass ceiling profession for black people. The only way to advance was to assimilate or start your own engineering firm and I had no interest in doing neither.

CONCLUSIONS

1. Working for black people is just as bad as working for white people.
2. I don't know what to believe in.
3. Black people will never be justly compensated for their work.
4. Never quit because my mother never quit.
5. The only way I will ever be truly successful and acquire wealth is to establish something on my own. Because, a black man can never excel in Corporate America unless he assimilates (sells out).

11

Well Done Mama

A mother's death, however, is potentially an even more powerful change in a son's life. Dr. Lifton believes that "The loss of one's mother is perceived more as the loss of someone one has experienced intimate love for—or at least a more immediate love."
... A recent English study suggests that a mother's death may be more traumatic than the father's for adult children of both sexes. But this same study suggests that the effects may be especially intense for sons. Mardi Horowitz, an American psychiatrist, wrote in an "Archives of General Psychiatry" article that both sons and daughters seem to find a mother's death harder to tolerate. The possible explanation is that mother's have generally been the primary caregivers for children, so that mother-child attachments are often stronger than father-child attachments. (45)

-Edward Myers, When Parents Die

Pour out some liquor and I reminsce,
cuz through the drama,
I can always depend on my mama
And when it seems that I'm hopeless,
You say the words that can get me back in focus
When I was sick as a little kid,
To keep me happy there's no limit to the things you did
And all my childhood memories,
Are full of all the sweet things you did for me
And even though I act craaazy,
I gotta thank the Lord that you made me
There are no words that can express how I feel,
You never kept a secret, always stayed real
And I appreciate, how you raised me,
And all the extra love that you gave me
I wish I could take the pain away,
If you can make it through the night there's a brighter day
Everything will be alright if ya hold on,

It's a struggle everyday, gotta roll on
And there's no way I can pay you back,
But my plan is to show you that I understand
You are appreciated

-Tupac Shakur, Dear Mama

24 YEARS OLD

Pick Your Head Up

As time went on, my mother's condition grew worse. She underwent several surgeries and several blood transfusions. The cancer had spread to her skin and to several of her vital organs. My father didn't tell me at the time but whenever he took my mother to the hospital for treatments or a check up, the doctors would give her a negative report and inform her that she didn't have much time left to live. She would respond by saying, "God hasn't told me that."

She always ended up out-living their predictions. The whole church knew my mother's story and every time they received a report that she wasn't doing well they wouldn't expect to see her in church. But every time the doors of the church would open on a Sunday morning for service or on a Wednesday evening for Bible Study, my mother would be one of the first people to walk through the doors to take her seat.

One evening at Bible Study after she had endured a grueling day of treatments she stood up to give a testimony. At this time my father was a deacon in training and he had to sit up front with the other deacons and face the congregation during Bible Study. As my mother spoke her voice trembled, not because of fear but because of the pain that she was enduring. She said the following,

> *"The doctors continue to tell me that I don't have long to live but I keep telling them they don't know the God I serve. Every time I say that they smile at me as if I'm crazy but I'm praying for them. I always end up arguing with them because they continue to diagnose me based on their medical intuition but I try to explain to them that my faith is not in their knowledge or their medicine but in my God."*

The more she spoke, the more the people in the congregation began to shout. But the more she spoke the sadder I became. I eventually put my head down because tears started to roll down my face. Then, I looked up and saw my father staring at me. He had tears in his eyes as well and he spoke to me. I couldn't hear his voice but I could read his lips and what he said was "Pick your head up."

God is Good

During one of my mother's routine check-ups, the doctors noticed a tumor growing on her throat. My mother was too weak to endure another surgery but they informed her that if she didn't allow them to perform the surgery and remove the tumor then she would lose her ability to speak.

After discussing it with my father she decided to go ahead and let them perform the surgery. I was at work waiting for my father to call me to let me know how the surgery turned out. He never called, so I left work early and went to the hospital to see what was going on.

When I arrived at the hospital and met with my dad he informed me that my mother's lungs had collapsed during the surgery. As a result of her lungs collapsing, the doctor's had to perform an emergency tracheotomy, which involved cutting a hole in her throat and inserting a tube so that she could breathe. She almost died.

When I walked into her room to see her, she was sitting up but she couldn't talk and the only way that she could communicate was to write on a notebook. She saw the anger on my face and wrote on her notebook, "Terrence, what's wrong?" I didn't respond and I just shook my head. My mother could read me like a book and she could tell that I was losing faith.

She smiled at me and began to write in her notebook again and this time she wrote, "Terrence, God is good." I stayed in the hospital with her that night because I thought that she was going to die and I didn't want her to die alone. She didn't die and she ended up staying awake most of the night watching me sleep.

25 YEARS OLD

Bloody T-Shirts

Over time, my mother's skin cancer began to cause sores and boils on her body. The sores and boils would burst at night while she slept and when she woke in the morning her t-shirt would be stained with blood. Sometimes her t-shirts were so bloody that she would have to change them in the middle of the night.

She never complained, but I did on the inside, and my facial expressions told it all. Sometimes I would even look to the sky and frown. It got to the point where I wondered if God even cared because it didn't seem like He did to me.

I Look Like A Monster

Later on, my mother also developed an infection due to all of the different medications that she was taking which caused her face to swell. There were times that her face would swell so much that you could barely make out her nose from her lips. As a result of the swelling, she began to have panic attacks whenever she looked at herself in the mirror.

Whenever her face would swell up to the point where she couldn't make out her facial features she would begin to scream and say, "I look like a monster!" My father would hold her and not allow her to continue to look at herself in the mirror. He would console her and let her know that she was still beautiful and that the swelling would eventually go down in time.

I could barely believe what I was seeing and the more I saw my mother suffer the more upset I became with God. I began to wonder to myself, *"Why is God taking her through all of this and if He is not going to heal her then why doesn't He just take her to heaven?"*

This Is My Cross

Every morning my mother would wake up coughing and gagging for about thirty minutes trying to clear her throat of the bile and mucus that built up in her lungs as she slept. The cancer had infected several of her organs, including her liver, thus causing the mucus build up in her lungs.

I used to pat her on the back to help her clear her throat but she would tell me to stop because it didn't help. She tried to comfort me by saying that this was just something she had to endure.

Oftentimes, she would tell people, "This is my cross and I have to bear it." After a while, I realized that my mother was never going to be cured of cancer so I stopped asking God to heal her and I started asking Him could He just take her home as painlessly as possible.

Let Me Dress You

The radiation therapy had caused my mother's bones and teeth to become brittle and a couple of her teeth had chipped. As a result, she used to cover her mouth when she smiled and she couldn't eat crunchy food, so she ate soup most of the time.

One day while my mother and I were sitting at the kitchen table eating, she began to tell me about this dream she had. She said in the dream a man came to her dressed in all white. She said the man began to take off her clothes and as he was taking off her clothes he began to say, "Let me dress you, let me dress you." She told me that after he had taken off her old dirty clothes he put all new white clothing on her just like his clothing.

Later on after that story, my mother tried on several occasions to sit me down and go over her insurance papers but I never would talk to her about it. Then one day she looked me in my eyes and said, "Terrence, please don't ever forget me."

2002 Women's Day Conference

My mother was one of five women selected from our church to speak at their annual Women's Day Conference. The theme for their conference was "UNITY" and each of the five women was given one of the letters from the word "UNITY" to speak on. My mother was given the last letter "Y" and from the letter "Y" my mother wrote her speech about the word "Yield".

She was very fatigued and weak while she was studying and preparing for her speech and she didn't know whether she would have enough strength to deliver it on the day of the conference.

However, despite her fatigue, on Friday, May 17, 2002, the day of the conference she was as resilient as ever and after all of the other women had given their speeches she was the last person who had to speak. The treatments that she had endured just days before took a major toll on her body and as she approached the podium trembling, she opened up with the following words:

> *"It's been a rough week for me. I had a whole day of cancer treatments on Tuesday. Body wracked with pain on Wednesday. I had to get two blood transfusions Thursday, and I asked God am I going to be able to come out Lord and speak for You? Do I need to call and tell them to get someone else? He didn't answer me, so apparently it was meant for me to come out to speak, you know (Applause). So I ask you to just please bear with me. If I be slow and if my voice trembles I want to do it for the Lord because I may not get another chance to do this." (Applause)*

As she began her speech her voice was real low and frail but the more she spoke the louder and more powerful her voice became. After she finished her speech, the audience gave her a standing ovation. When she made it back home she was drained and went right to sleep.

No More Pain

On Wednesday, May 22, 2002 I went into the hospital to have reconstructive knee surgery because I had torn my ACL playing football the year prior. After the surgery, the pain was unbearable and I couldn't walk.

My mother went back into the hospital the next day, on Thursday, for a check-up. My father called me at home and said that she had an infection so the doctors decided to keep her overnight so they could treat her and she would be back home on Friday. When Friday came, my mother called me to see how I was doing and she told me that the doctors said that they needed her to stay at the hospital for another night and that she should be home on Saturday. The last thing that she said to me before we got off of the phone was, *"Terrence, I love you."*

The next day, my younger brother and I were watching the NBA conference finals. After the game went off around 8:00pm, I realized that I hadn't heard from my mother or my father all day. I called her room and somebody picked up her phone and hung it up without saying anything. So I called back and somebody picked up the phone and hung it up again.

I didn't know what was going on so I called the main desk and asked to be transferred to Betty Jones' room and the nurse responded, "Sir we're doing everything we can for her right now." I asked, "What are you talking about?" She said that she couldn't go into details. I told her to find my father, Sherman Jones, and put him on the phone.

When my father got on the phone I asked him what was going on and he said that my mother was not doing well. I told him I was on the way and he told me not to come because I couldn't drive. I hung up on him. I told my brother to get his clothes on so we could leave.

My father had called our next door neighbor and he came over and told me that he would give me a ride to the hospital because he didn't want me to drive. On the way to the hospital, he could see that I was pissed off with my dad because he didn't call me and let me know what was going on. He told me to do him a favor and take it easy on my dad because he is really going through right now. I didn't respond.

When my brother and I made it to the cancer ward, we turned down the main hallway leading to my mother's room and at the end of the hallway we saw our father walking toward us. He had his hands in his pockets and there were two nurses walking with him (one nurse on each side). He looked up and saw us and as we got closer he put his head down. When we finally got close enough to him I asked him how was she doing and he just shook his head. So I asked him again in a louder voice, "How is she doing?" and he said that she didn't make it.

My brother ran away and started crying and I turned around on my crutches and started to walk away. Then, I stopped and told them to take me to her. When I reached her room, I saw her lying on the bed and I just fell on the bed beside her and started screaming, "Ma! Ma! Ma!" I couldn't stop crying.

A few minutes later they brought my brother in the room and he broke down as well. After a while, I pulled myself together and sat in the chair next to her bed and just stared at her. I couldn't believe that she was gone. I was devastated but at the same time I was relieved because I could see that she wasn't in anymore pain.

More Bad News

My family came in from out of town to help us plan my mother's funeral. I needed to get away, so I took a trip to visit my friend Kevin who was still in prison. I wanted to tell him face-to-face about my mother passing. When I got to the visitors room, he could see that I was on crutches and he asked me why I drove over an hour to see him on crutches. That is when I told him about my mother and he started to cry.

I didn't cry because I wanted him to know that I was doing okay. As we talked, he told me that he had heard that my ex-girlfriend had a baby about two months ago. It didn't faze me at first, but on the drive back home the news hit me like a ton of bricks and I broke down in the car.

When I made it to my house, I went straight to my room and closed the door. I laid on my bed and started crying. My aunt came into the room to check on me and saw that I was upset. I told her about the news I had just received and she asked me if I planned on getting back with my ex-girlfriend. I told her no, that I didn't, and as a matter of fact I hadn't even been thinking about her. However, at that moment I was just vulnerable and that news, on top of the pain in my knee and my mother's death was just too much to bear.

My aunt told me that I was going to have to soldier it out because everybody in the family was looking to me for support. She said that the family couldn't lean on my dad because he had just lost his soul mate and couldn't support us. They couldn't lean on my brother because he was the baby, so therefore the lot fell on me. I told her that I couldn't do it and she said, "Yes you can." I asked her how she knew that I could carry the load and she said that I could carry it because I didn't have a choice.

She also said that she would help me as much as she could but in the end, I was on my own. When she left out of my room, I prayed to God to give me the strength to endure and He strengthened me at that very moment.

Well Done Mama

On the day of my mother's funeral, I drove up to the church by myself about two hours before the funeral so I could sit alone with her. I wanted to get all of my crying out before everybody showed up. When I saw her in the casket, she was a shade darker like my grandmother was but her face looked full and she didn't even look like she had been sick. I was happy about that.

I held her hand and kissed her. That was the first time I had ever touched someone in a casket. She wasn't cold like I thought she would be. She was actually warm. After I talked to her for a little while, I ended by telling her that I will always love her and that I will never forget her. Then I went back home and sat with my family.

I wrote a poem that I inserted into my mother's program that I planned to read at the funeral. My younger brother, who was fifteen years old at the time, read one of my mother's favorite Scripture passages (Psalm 91). I was extremely proud of him for being strong enough to stand up in front of everyone and read that Scripture because that was something that I probably wouldn't have been strong enough to do when I was his age.

Later on, I went up to read the poem. Normally I would have been scared to death to speak publicly, but on that day there was not a demon in hell that would have kept me from reading that poem. I made up my mind to read that poem, even if I stuttered on every word. The title of the poem was *"Well Done Mama."*

I didn't stutter one time as I got up to address the people and read the poem. After I finished, everybody stood up on their feet and applauded. My mother was a soldier and fought cancer tooth and nail. In the end, she didn't even die from cancer but from kidney failure. She went twelve rounds with the Big C and won. Well Done, Mama. Well Done.

"His Lord said unto him, Well done, thou good and faithful servant: thou hast been faithful over a few things, I will make thee ruler over many things: enter thou into the joy of thy Lord."
–Matthew 25:21

CONCLUSIONS

1. It's not fair for my mother to suffer so other people can be inspired.
2. If God is so good, then why is He allowing my mother to suffer so much?
3. God doesn't really care about us.
4. If God is not going to heal my mother, then He should have mercy and take her home.
5. Prayer doesn't really work because God is only going to do what is in His will to do.
6. Mama, I will never forget you or the suffering you went through.
7. Despite whatever pain you are enduring, you still have to fulfill your obligations, especially to God.
8. I have to stand because if I fall so will everybody else.
9. Mama is in a better place, a place without any pain.

Half Time:

Reflection and Recovery

12

Reflection: Understanding the Past

A National Institutes of Health study suggests that the region of the brain that inhibits risky behavior is not fully formed until age 25, a finding with implications for a host of policies, including the nation's driving laws..."We'd thought the highest levels of physical and brain maturity were reached by age 18, maybe earlier -- so this threw us," said Jay Giedd, a pediatric psychiatrist leading the study, which released its first results in April. That makes adolescence "a dangerous time, when it should be the best."

-Brain Immaturity Could Explain Teen Crash Rate
by Elizabeth Williamson

"5. The cortex is the top layer of the brain and is about the depth of two dimes placed on top of each other. The cortex is the "executive branch" of the brain that regulates decision-making and controls thinking, reasoning and language.

The cerebral cortex contains 80 percent of the neurons in the brain. Because it is the least developed part of the brain at birth and keeps developing until adolescence and even beyond, the cortex is more sensitive to experiences than other parts of the brain.

Construction of the brain is somewhat like the construction of a house. A house is built from the foundation up and different parts of the structure have different functions. Also, like the brain, once the architecture is in place, you can continue learning and "add on" or "decorate." But, if you have to move a wall or add a window, it is more difficult and expensive than if you had done it earlier in the building process."

-Understanding Brain Development in Young Children
by Sean Brotherson

I chose to entitle this portion of the book *"Half-Time"* because I want to use this section to reflect on the first half of the book and to set the stage for the second half. Similarly, at any sporting event there is a point in the game where the team takes a break and goes back into the locker room and discusses their performance in the first half.

If the team is currently winning, then they pretty much can stick with the game plan at hand. But, good coaches will always look for areas where the team can improve. However, if the team is losing then the coaching staff has to go back to the drawing board and determine what they need to do differently to change the outcome of the game.

During the course of my life, I have experienced several traumatic events as detailed in the first half. As a result of those experiences, I developed a negative outlook on life. After each experience, I came to some sort of conclusion about life and most of those conclusions were negative.

These conclusions served as laws that I lived by which protected me for a season but over time these same laws hindered me from becoming truly successful because I was operating in a spirit of fear and pessimism. Every time I had a bad experience and drew a negative conclusion it became another steel bar that was set in place to imprison my mind and cause me to believe that I was incapable of achieving anything of great significance.

Whenever I had an idea, this negative mindset always caused me to focus on the obstacles instead of the possibilities. These so-called obstacles put me in a state of paralysis, and I wouldn't move. After a while, I would end up putting that idea on the shelf with all of the other ideas that I had but was too afraid to put into action. In the end, all of my dreams were just sitting in my mind collecting dust.

There were several factors that were the catalyst for my condition that I had no control over; namely, my critical and abusive father, hostile environment (in and out of school), terminally ill mother, deaths of family members, racism, etc.

These all came to a head at the passing of my mother when I was twenty-five years old. According to the research stated above, the highest level of brain maturity happens at the age of twenty-five and the development of your brain is similar to the construction of a house. Once it is built, it is more difficult and costly to then go back and make major renovations.

Well, in my case, my brain was constructed on a foundation of trauma and by the time I turned twenty-five it had become a structure of concrete negativity reinforced by steel bars of hopelessness.

After my mother passed away, I began to drift away from God. I still continued to go to church but my faith in God had faltered. I was serving God out of obligation and duty instead of serving Him out of love and sincere devotion.

After seeing my mother suffer from cancer and eventually die, I just couldn't wrap my mind around why God would allow her to go through such an ordeal. Furthermore, my stuttering condition was getting worse and it seemed like no matter how hard I prayed to God and how long I fasted that God was just not listening to me. I began to believe that God wasn't concerned about me so I began to withdraw from Him.

Up until that point, I had practiced abstinence for over three and a half years but eventually I began to self-medicate by using sex. I was torn because whenever I fornicated, which occurred sporadically throughout the year, I never enjoyed it because I would get convicted. Then the guilt from my sin would cause me to withdraw even further away from God. I was lost.

One day when I came home from work, I saw a baby bird in my driveway. I immediately went into the house and retrieved a shoebox to put him in because I was going to take him to the local animal shelter. I figured that he had fallen out of his nest and injured himself.

Before I took him to the animal shelter, I decided to call first to let them know that I was going to drop off the bird in case they needed to give me some instructions on how to handle the bird before I dropped him off.

When the receptionist answered the phone, I informed her about the bird and told her that I wanted to bring him in and she told me that before I did she wanted to ask me a few questions. I said okay. She asked me was the bird fully feathered. I said I'm not a bird expert but it appears to me that he has all of his feathers. Then she said, well if he does then there is nothing that we can do for him so please do not bring him to the shelter. I asked her why not and she said that he didn't fall out of his nest but he was bumped out of his nest by his parents.

In utter disbelief, I asked her why. She said they bumped him out of the nest because he should be flying by now and they have to make room for their next batch of eggs. I asked, "Well what I am supposed to do with him?" She told me to put him back where I found him. I then asked her what is going to happen to him. She said that he will either fly or he is going to die.

She also said that his parents will bring him food for a while but eventually he is going to have to fly because he is vulnerable on the ground. The longer he stays there, the greater the chance a predator will come along to kill and eat him. It is going to be harder for him to take flight from the ground versus from the nest but he can do it if he believes in himself. He has allowed his fear of trying to cause him to sit back and just wait for his parents to feed him. If he wants to live, then his only option is to fly. I said, "Wow, that's rough." She replied, "Hey, that's life."

I realized that God sent that bird to me to let me know that I needed to get myself together or else I was going to end up like that bird; bumped out of God's grace and walking the streets of depression and apathy.

Just like that bird I had everything I needed to take flight and accomplish the things that God had revealed to me, but the baggage in my mind was weighing me down and I didn't believe in myself or my abilities. I was focusing too much on my weaknesses, or should I say, my perceived weaknesses versus my strengths. I needed to alleviate myself of this dead weight in my mind so that I could take flight.

Sitting around blaming God, my father, society, and my traumatic experiences for my inability to achieve my dreams was not the answer and the longer I did this, the more vulnerable I became to depression and resorting back to my old way of life. Somehow, someway, I was going to have to change the way I was thinking because my mind had become my greatest enemy. This was leading to my downfall.

"For as he (a man) thinketh in his heart, so is he:" **–Proverbs 23:7**

13

Recovery: Unearthing Your Purpose

Proverbs 25:2 – It is the glory of God to conceal a thing; but the honour of kings is to search out a matter.

The Scripture noted above, Proverbs 25:2, is the central theme of the entire book. I came across this Scripture years ago when I first gave my life to Christ and for some reason it stuck with me. After carefully studying it, God revealed to me its true meaning.

It is similar to an Easter egg hunt that you would have with your kids during the Easter holiday. You boil a whole carton of eggs and then you decorate them only to go outside and hide them from your kids. The goal is for your kids to go out and find the eggs. As they search for the eggs, you guide them along and give them advice until they finally find them. Once they do, everybody is happy.

Now you could have just as easily given your kids the eggs but the excitement and joy of the event is not in the eggs themselves but in the pursuit of the eggs.

That is what God does with us regarding our purpose in life. God conceals our destiny and instructs and guides us by His Word and His Holy Spirit to help us navigate through the ups and downs of life until we finally discover who we are called to be. He does this so we can become accustomed to hearing His voice and obeying Him rather than depending on ourselves.

During the journey, He allows us to experience different things which, when put into proper perspective, is really a tool that He has given us to be used at some later time in our lives. The joy and fulfillment of life is not in your final destination or achieving your purpose, but in the journey to reach that destination. The journey is what develops your character so whenever you come into your purpose, you will be properly equipped to carry it out as God intends.

Furthermore, as it pertains to Proverbs 25:2, kings are not born but they are made. They are made and refined in the furnace of affliction. This is why the Scripture states, *"but the honour of kings is to search out a matter."* It is only when you endure the trials of life and conquer them that you can then receive power from God to carry out your destiny.

A king is any person who can survive the ups and downs of life and use them to his or her advantage. A king is not ruled by their hardships or circumstances, nor do they bow down in defeat to them. But a king overcomes them and conquers every test set before them as God gives them authority to do so.

Kings are given this authority as they obey God and diligently examine the many different stages of their lives and inquire of God, who then gives them understanding as to why He had to take them through certain wilderness experiences.

The principles of Proverbs 25:2 are best illustrated in the life of Joseph. You can read about his story in the book of Genesis, Chapters 37 and 39-50.

To briefly summarize Joseph's story, he was given two dreams by God and the ability to interpret these dreams at the age of seventeen. In each dream, God showed Joseph that his family would bow down to him. He then told his family members about his dreams and they became upset.

Afterwards, Joseph's brothers sold him into slavery but later he became a servant to a wealthy Egyptian named Potiphar, who was one of Pharaoh's officials and captain of the guard. Due to his devotion to God and his diligent work ethic, he was promoted and put in charge of everything in Potiphar's house.

One day, Potiphar's wife vigorously made sexual advances toward Joseph, but he resisted as usual. However, on this particular day she wasn't taking no for an answer. All Joseph could do was run out of the house but Potiphar's wife kept a piece of his clothing. She then accused Joseph of sexually assaulting her. Upon hearing this news, Potiphar became furious and had Joseph thrown into prison.

God was with Joseph and because of Joseph's devotion to God and his administrative abilities he was promoted once again and put in charge of the entire prison. At this point, he was twenty-eight years old and had been estranged from his family for eleven years when two of Pharaoh's officials were sent to the prison under Joseph's supervision.

One of the officials was Pharaoh's chief butler and the other official was Pharaoh's chief baker. Both of these individuals had dreams that troubled them and Joseph volunteered to interpret their dreams. In the end, the chief butler was eventually restored to his position but the chief baker was executed.

Joseph told the chief butler to remember him and to put in a good word for him with Pharaoh because he was an innocent man and sought to be released from prison. It would be another two years before the chief butler would remember Joseph and mention him to Pharaoh.

After two years, Pharaoh had a dream that none of his magicians and soothsayers could interpret and the chief butler remembered Joseph and they had him brought to Pharaoh. By the Spirit of God, Joseph was able to interpret Pharaoh's dream and as a result, Egypt was able to put together a plan to store up food for a severe famine that was going to overtake the land for seven years. Pharaoh then promoted Joseph and Joseph became the most powerful man in Egypt and second in command only to Pharaoh himself.

People from all across the region traveled to Egypt to get food as a result of the famine. One day, Joseph noticed that his brothers were among those who needed food. His brothers didn't recognize him but he recognized them and after testing the devotion of his brothers he eventually revealed his true identity to them. He then told them to bring his father's family to stay with him in Egypt. This eventually led to the entire nation of Israel migrating to Egypt and settling in the region of Goshen.

After the death of their father, Joseph's brothers were terrified because they thought Joseph had spared their lives because of their father but figured that since their father was dead Joseph would seek revenge for selling him into slavery. Joseph reassured his brothers that he was not going to harm them because he realized that all of what he had been through was part of God's plan for his life. Genesis 50:19-21 states:

> "[19]And Joseph said unto them, Fear not: for am I in the place of God? [20]But as for you, ye thought evil against me; but God meant it unto good, to bring to pass, as it is this day, to save much people alive. [21]Now therefore fear ye not: I will nourish you, and your little ones. And he comforted them, and spake kindly unto them."

God used slavery and prison to develop Joseph into an excellent administrator and a wise ruler. God's methods have not changed and He uses those same methods today to develop us as well.

Every human being is born with gifts and talents. Many people believe that gifts and talents are the same but they're not. Talent is a person's natural inclination to be good at something. Talent is developed over time and can be enhanced by the individual through extensive practice and discipline. Gifts on the other hand cannot be developed solely by sheer hard work and dedication but they are given only by God and can be developed only by maintaining a spiritual connection to God.

Joseph's gift was interpreting dreams which he could only perform by the power of God but his talents were administration and supervision, which were developed through his trials. As stated in Proverbs 18:16, *"A man's gift maketh room for him, and bringeth him before great men."* Joseph's gift of interpreting dreams ushered him into Pharaoh's presence but his talents allowed him to be promoted to achieve his destiny of ruling a nation and saving the lives of his countrymen.

After studying the life of Joseph, I realized that God had plans to use my circumstances to develop my character, which would enable me to carry out my purpose. As a result, I heeded the call and embarked on the journey that God had mapped out for me.

The second half of this book will detail the journey that God led me on and how He showed me that there was a purpose for all of the traumatic events that I experienced in my life.

"[11]'For I know the plans that I have for you,' declares the LORD, 'plans for welfare and not for calamity to give you a future and a hope." (NASB) –Jeremiah 29:11

3rd Quarter:

Road

to

Recovery

-14-

New Wine

Matthew 9:16-17 – [16]*"But no one puts a patch of unshrunk cloth on an old garment; for the patch pulls away from the garment, and a worse tear results.* [17]*"Nor do people put new wine into old wineskins; otherwise the wineskins burst, and the wine pours out and the wineskins are ruined; but they put new wine into fresh wineskins, and both are preserved." (NASB)*

Old Wine Skins

[9]*He was also saying to them, "You are experts at setting aside the commandment of God in order to keep your tradition...* [13]*thus invalidating the word of God by your tradition which you have handed down; and you do many things such as that." (NASB)*
–Mark 7:9, 13

Before my mother passed away, I had told her on several occasions that I was thinking about leaving the church because I wasn't growing spiritually. The messages that were being taught were catered more towards the older people, who were entrenched in their traditions. The average age of the men that attended the church were in their mid-forties and up. I was one of the only men who consistently attended and served in the church that was in their twenties.

Due to the lack of young men in the church, I became the poster child for the young people and I was called on to serve on several different ministries. I was getting burnt out and the messages didn't relate to me. The only thing that I got satisfaction out of was teaching in the Youth Ministry. However, that didn't last too long because their youth curriculum wasn't relevant to many of the challenges that the young people were facing. The overseers of the program were too rigid and didn't want to come outside the box.

The only reason I stayed as long as I did was my mother begged me not to leave because she said that the youth needed me. My younger brother was also another reason why I hung around because he was in the youth class that I taught.

During one of our annual men's retreats one of the ministers got up to teach and he informed the men that he was going to share a story with them about something that he did that he wasn't too proud of. Naturally the men were on the edge of their seats because the ministers rarely shared anything about themselves when they taught and if they did, it was surface.

He said that when he was a young boy one of his closest family members passed away and after it happened he was very upset with God and confused. A few days later, as he was walking home, he passed this farm and saw a chicken walking around. He said that he had so much pent up anger and frustration that he picked up a stick and threw it and killed the chicken.

After killing the chicken, he went home and started crying and asked God to forgive him because he realized that he had sinned. When he finished telling that story, all of the men started laughing. I didn't attend that men's retreat but when they told me that story I said to myself,

> *"A chicken! You mean to tell me that one of the worst things he has done is kill a damn chicken. I don't give a damn about no damn chickens. Killing chickens don't mean a damn thing to me. We eat chickens."*

I know, I sound like my dad. Now I'm not trying to belittle the man's story or the pain that he experienced at the loss of his loved one but what's the truth? I'm pretty sure that he has done some things far worse than killing a chicken. But he was religious and religion requires you to cover up and hide.

However, you can't reach people that way. You have to be real and share your dirt and how you missed the mark and then tell how God redeemed you from your sins. This is what inspires people to overcome their struggles.

After my mother passed away, I stayed about two more months but then I ended up leaving and attending another church. My prayer was, "God please send me to a church where there are some men my age who are serious about serving You that can help me grow spiritually." I prayed this prayer because I was lost and had begun to drift back into some bad habits.

Put it on the Glass

[22]To the weak became I as weak, that I might gain the weak: I am made all things to all men, that I might by all means save some.
−1 Corinthians 9:22

In the summer of 2002, shortly after the passing of my mother, a friend of mine who used to attend our church invited me to visit his church. The following Sunday morning, I got up and put on my Sunday's best and when I got to his church I realized that I was overdressed. Everybody had regular clothes on and even the Pastor had a football jersey on with some blue jeans.

It was a culture shock for me and the church was packed with young black men my age. I became nervous because the only time I had ever seen that many black men in one place was at the club and normally a fight would break out. I began to brace myself thinking that I was going to get into an altercation. That's how sick I was. Even though I was saved, I still had a street mentality and didn't trust people.

There was nothing traditional about this church. I didn't know how to act. I didn't know any of the songs that they were singing and they didn't have any hymn books so that I could follow along. So, I just stood there in utter disbelief. I felt like a fish out of water. When the Pastor got up to preach he didn't hold anything back. I couldn't believe some of the things that he was saying. He put it on the glass.

Now some of you might not know what *"put it on the glass"* means but let me explain. *"Put it on the glass,"* is a term that is used at the strip club that signifies baring everything and getting up close and personal. That's how he taught. He bared everything and he shared his personal business. Hey! What can I say? I haven't always been saved.

Anyway, as he taught he would constantly make references to his life. He talked about how he used to smoke weed, do cocaine, fornicate, steal, etc. He was totally transparent as he preached the Gospel and so were all of the other ministers that he trained.

The theme of their church was *"Keeping it Real"* and that is what they did. The original name of the church was, *"Church of the Lord's Disciples"* but after a couple of years the leadership decided that that name sounded too religious so they renamed the church, *"The Soul Factory."*

The Pastor didn't even allow people to call him Pastor but he let people address him by his name, Deron. He lowered himself and made himself like one of us so that we could relate to his message and receive the truth which was that God can save and redeem anyone, no matter what they have done.

God answered my prayers and sent me to a place that served new wine. I had found a new church that could relate to me and from that day on, I have never looked back.

I'm Laying Low

[6]Do not claim honor in the presence of the king, And do not stand in the place of great men; [7]For it is better that it be said to you, "Come up here, "Than for you to be placed lower in the presence of the prince, (NASB) **–Proverbs 25:6-7a**

Despite the fact that God answered my prayers and sent me to a church that ministered to my needs, I was reluctant to serve on any of their ministries. The reason for this was I burnt out from serving at my old church. Also, I never knew if I was elevated at that church because I was the only young man there and because my father was a deacon or was I truly elevated by God.

Therefore, when I began attending my new church, I made up my mind not to join any ministries and to wait and see what God would have me to do. I knew that I had the gift of teaching, but I didn't make mention of that to anyone. I prayed to God and asked Him that if I was truly called to serve then He would have to show me. Until then, I was going to lay low.

The first thing that some people do when they attend a new church is try to get in good with the leadership so they can be promoted. Not me. I'm not like that at all and I don't do clichés. I figured if God wants me to serve Him in some major capacity, then He will open the door. But, it is not my job to be up in the Pastor's face trying to get some recognition.

I did help out from time-to-time but I never committed myself to anything. The only thing that I did was join a cell group, which is a gender based small group of people that meet bi-weekly to have bible studies and fellowships. Cell groups are the core of the church because they help people to build relationships. Other than that, I would go to church to hear the Word and give my offering. After service was over, I would roll out. This went on for over a year.

2003 Man-Up Weekend

¹So David got away and escaped to the Cave of Adullam. When his brothers and others associated with his family heard where he was, they came down and joined him. ² Not only that, but all who were down on their luck came around—losers and vagrants and misfits of all sorts. David became their leader. (The Message)
−1 Samuel 22:1-2a

In the fall of 2003, Deron announced that we were going to have a men's retreat that he called *"Man-Up."* Man-Up took place on a fifty-eight acre retreat center that the church owned called, Another Way Challenge Center.

I didn't really know that many people, but I still signed up to go. As usual, I kept to myself. Our team's first event was the obstacle course. I already knew that I was going to blaze through the course and have one of the shortest times. Sports have always been my comfort zone because I was naturally athletic and I always maintained a consistent weight training regiment.

When it was my turn to go through the course, I blazed through the course as expected, but at the very end of the course I sprained my ankle. I could barely walk and I had to be helped off the field. People had to attend to me and it felt awkward because I was not used to letting anyone help me. After they wrapped my ankle, I limped back to my campsite.

A couple of the guys on my team carried my bags for me and brought me my food. I never experienced anything like this in my life, black men looking out for each other. I realized later that God allowed me to sprain my ankle to humble me and teach me that it's okay to be vulnerable and allow people to help me.

After a while, I started to let my guards down and began to talk to different people and I found out that we all had similar stories. It was over two hundred and fifty men in attendance and there was a mixture of Ex-murderers, drug dealers, thieves, junkies, alcoholics, womanizers, etc. Despite everyone's background, we all had one thing in common and that was we were all seeking God and wisdom on how to improve our lives and the lives of our families.

When Deron taught at the sessions, he discussed many of the issues affecting the black community and tied them to the Bible. He taught that our plight was also the Lord's plight and that God had not forgotten about us. He emphasized that we could not wait on the government because the black community was a distant second on their agenda and we had to take responsibility for our own community and work together to save our people.

I'd never heard the Gospel taught like that before. I was fired up and ready to make a difference. The atmosphere was electric and the love and camaraderie among the men reminded me of the Civil Rights movement in the sixties. My spirit was quickened and I wanted all the men that I knew to have this type of experience.

When I got home, I purchased every book that Deron mentioned at Man-Up because he always stresses that we need to read and I began to study like a madman. Once I returned back to the church, I joined the security ministry. Not too long after that I was one of the overseers of security. Man didn't elevate me but God did.

Rites of Passage Summer Camp

[6]Train up a child in the way he should go: and when he is old, he will not depart from it. **—Proverbs 22:6**

Later on in the spring of 2004, Deron announced that the church was going to launch it's first *"Rites of Passage Summer Camp."* The church was known for its annual summer camp but this was the first time that they would conduct a rites of passage summer camp.

On several occasions, Deron expressed his desire to implement a rites of passage program for the youth in the black community. In his book, *"How to love a Black Man,"* Deron wrote:

*"In the Jewish culture, a boy is given a ceremony called a Bar Mitzvah. This ceremony is his introduction into manhood by his family, whereas the black boy has no sort of rites of passage. The rites a black boy receives are the rites of **depersonalization**. That is the stripping away of your manhood, personhood, individuality, and humanity, resulting in a male adult whose only desire in life is to make himself happy."(51-52)*

Deron announced that he needed some men to work the camp, so I signed up. At this time, I was in the process of resigning from engineering because I had just received my real estate license and I was currently in the process of getting my real estate appraiser's trainee license. So, I had the time to devote to the camp. Plus, I was still on fire from Man-Up, so I was down for whatever.

When the camp began, they assigned me to the youngest group; the seven and eight year olds. What I didn't know then was that this was the worst group in the bunch. The maximum attention span of a seven to eight year old is approximately ten minutes and after that, all bets are off. Those kids ended up driving me crazy.

In addition to that, the group leader that I was partnered with had doctor's appointments every other day so I would be all alone to supervise the kids. It seemed like he would come to me everyday and say, "Hey T, I have a doctor's appointment today. So, what I'll do is take care of the boys in the morning and then when I leave, you can take over in the afternoon." I said to myself, *"Watching them in the morning is easy because they're not awake yet but by the time the afternoon get's here, they will be in rare form."*

I was getting tired of him and his doctor's appointments and it got to the point where I wanted to tell him, *"Why don't you just go ahead and die already, so that way they can hire somebody else to take your place that is going to help me with these kids."* Yeah, I know that that thought was wicked but I needed help and those kids were draining my soul.

Every other weekend we would take the kids to Another Way Challenge Center (AWCC) to spend the weekend. Of course on the weekend that we had the most kids in our group, which was a total of thirty-six boys; my partner couldn't make it because he had a doctor's appointment. I had two youth counselors working with me but they weren't that much help, because the kids didn't listen to them. Therefore, I was on my own.

I had to mobilize thirty-six kids for two days straight by myself. I had to teach them, feed them, and make sure they took showers and went to bed. A couple of them were scared of the dark and came in the room where I was sleeping and I had to let them sleep in my bed while I slept on the floor. My prayer became, *"Lord, please help me to survive this summer camp."*

There was one kid in particular who was brilliant and always raised his hands to participate in the class discussions. The only problem was that he was very annoying to the other kids because they felt that he was a know-it-all. When I wasn't around the other kids would beat him up. He was always a target because he wore thick glasses and he also wore his camp shorts so high that they were just below his navel.

Everyday he would come to me and say, "Mr. Terrence, they keep picking on me." Finally one day, I had it and I told him that he was going to have to start defending himself and if somebody hit him that he was going to have to hit them back. Yeah, yeah, yeah! I know that advice was not good Christian doctrine but so be it, I was exhausted.

The next day when his mom dropped him off, she came to me and asked me did I tell her son to hit people back who were picking on him. I thought to myself, *"Well, I'm about to be fired from summer camp for instructing one of the kids to fight. This could just very well be a blessing in disguise."* I told her yes, I did tell her son that he needed to learn to defend himself and to stop letting people pick on him.

After I confessed hoping that this may very well be my way out, she stuck her hand out and shook my hand and said thanks. She explained to me that she had been telling her son that he needed to start taking up for himself but he never listened to her. She said that night he came home and was proud of himself because he hit somebody back for the first time in his life. She said that he rarely sees his father, so spending time with the men in the camp was a blessing.

That's when I realized that despite the twelve hour days and the stress of dealing with those kids, I was making a difference in their lives. At the end of the camp, Deron shook my hand and told me congratulations; I was a real man because I survived summer camp. He said that most men don't make it through summer camp, but he was proud of me because I hung in there.

Anatomy of a Brother Who Raised Himself

[18]*Pride goeth before destruction, and an haughty spirit before a fall. –Proverbs 16:18*

The Soul Factory specializes in urban productions that depict the issues facing the black community through song, dance, poetry, and acting. Deron assembled a team of men to operate the special effects equipment for one of his plays, *"Anatomy of a Brother Who Raised Himself."* When he first assembled the team and met with us I took the initiative and did the layout for the effects, so he ended up making me the team leader.

Everything went smoothly at first. The rehearsals were going well and during the first couple of live performances of the production, we hit all of our cues and didn't miss a beat. As a result of our success, we began to get cocky.

Then it happened, one day a couple of the guys didn't show up and we were undermanned and we were scrambling at the last minute trying to get our equipment ready for that evening's performance. We were running around like chickens with our heads cut off. Deron warned us to stop moving so fast because he said that somebody was going to get hurt. We didn't listen and then he came back again and said, "Stop moving so fast and slow down because the Spirit told me that somebody is going to get hurt."

To make a long story short, during the production when we went to set off one of the effects, it blew up in one of my teammate's face. As a result of not listening, he almost lost his eyesight. The next day, Deron met with us and told us that we were prideful and needed to learn how to listen and follow instructions. I never realized that I was prideful, but after that incident I checked in and began to respect and revere the anointing that was on Deron's life and ministry.

TRUTH

1. There is no power in being religious, but only in being spiritual.
2. The only way to truly help to clean someone up is to share your dirt with them.
3. There is no hiding from God. If He is calling you, you will answer.
4. Black men can come together to worship God and make a difference in their communities.
5. God used the boys in the summer camp to make a man out of me.
6. God will always humble the prideful.

-15-

Boot Camp

Hebrews 12:11 – *[11]Now no chastening (discipline) for the present seemeth to be joyous, but grievous: nevertheless afterward it yieldeth the peaceable fruit of righteousness unto them which are exercised (trained) thereby.*

All Doors Closed Except One

[9]A man's heart deviseth his way: but the LORD directeth his steps.
–Proverbs 16:9

As soon as the Rites of Passage summer camp ended, I began to pursue my career in real estate and became a full-time real estate agent. Business was slow, but I managed to complete my first deal within three months. I was a buyer's agent for a friend of mine who purchased his first home. I had also just obtained my real estate appraiser trainee license and I was looking for work, but I couldn't find anyone to hire me.

My ultimate goal was to become a real estate developer, so I figured I needed to learn every aspect of the real estate game. That is why I started off as an agent and an appraiser. I wanted to learn how to buy and sell property; as well, as estimate property value.

At the end of 2004, I got a call from Deron's secretary saying that he wanted to meet with me. When I arrived at his office, he told me that he had prayed and God led him to ask me to come onboard and work with him in full-time ministry. He informed me that it wouldn't be easy and that I was in for the ride of my life, but he wanted me to pray on it.

A couple of months prior, I would have jumped at this opportunity. However, after working that summer camp and working with Deron during the production and enduring several of his corrections and rebukes, I wasn't really feeling it and I wanted to continue to pursue my real estate career.

I went to every appraisal company in the area and nobody was hiring. I spent over $1,500 in training and exams to get my real estate appraiser trainee license but I couldn't find a job to save my life. I had all of the credentials in the world, even an engineering background. It made no sense to me but then I realized that God had closed the doors leading to real estate and the only door that He left open was the one leading to ministry.

What Am I Doing Here?

[12]And if ye have not been faithful in that which is another man's, who shall give you that which is your own? –**Luke 16:12**

When I started to work in full-time ministry, I had no idea what I was called to do. I was initially brought on board to teach and train the men and the youth but that was put on hold.

In the beginning, all I did was assist Deron. I had to pick up his lunch, pick up his dry cleaning, get his cars washed, get his cars serviced, get stuff fixed at his house, drive him around town, accompany him on trips and carry his luggage.

My title was "Pastor's Armor Bearer," which simply means that you assist the pastor. Whenever family members or friends asked me what I did at work, I would tell them that I was an "Armor Bearer". They would ask me what did that mean and I would say, "I assist the pastor." Then, they would say, "Oh, you're an errand boy." To sum it up, that's what I was; an errand boy. Everyday I used to ask myself, *"What am I doing here?"* I was twenty-eight years old and I was picking up somebody else's dry cleaning for a living.

One day, I spoke with Deron and expressed my frustrations about my job and the menial tasks I was given. He explained to me that before God elevates a person, He first has to humble them. The way God humbles people is to have them serve someone else. He also said that before God will give a person the power to carry out their dreams, they must first help other people carry out theirs and in the process God will use that time to prepare them for their destiny.

Staff Meetings

[1]Whoever loves discipline loves knowledge, But he who hates reproof (correction) is stupid. (NASB) –**Proverbs 12:1**

We had staff meetings just about every other day and everybody dreaded them because it normally meant that somebody was about to get sternly rebuked for something they did wrong. Whenever it was announced that we were having a staff meeting, the first thing that came to my mind was, *"Oh Lord, what have I done wrong this time."*

When I first came on staff, I was the focus of several staff meetings. I was constantly getting rebuked but what made the situation so bad was that I was defensive and I couldn't accept correction. This was mainly because whenever I heard people correcting me or criticizing me, it reminded me of my father and that drove me crazy.

The thing that really used to aggravate me was when I was falsely accused of something. See, I'm not the type that is going to let somebody say something about me and not address what they said (especially if they are wrong) and there were a couple of times that I just didn't agree with what they were saying, so I had to speak up. That's how I'm made. I'm not a people pleaser.

After a while, Deron told me to do a study on rebukes and correction. When I did, I learned that as long as I walk in pride and refuse to humble myself and continue to resist correction, then the more I will stay stagnant and not grow.

I received his advice and I began to write down a few Scriptures about rebukes and corrections on index cards and read them before I went into staff meetings to prepare myself to be calm and just listen. I still didn't always agree with what they said, but I learned to accept whatever they said that was true and disregard what I felt wasn't true. I followed the saying, *"Chew up the meat and spit out the bones."*

Now I have to admit that they were right about 85% of the time but the other 15% of the time that they were wrong, I would only address if it was something major. If it was something minor, I would just let it ride.

God Sons

⁶Also, guide the young men to live disciplined lives. ⁷ But mostly, show them all this by doing it yourself, incorruptible in your teaching, ⁸ your words solid and sane. Then anyone who is dead set against us, when he finds nothing weird or misguided, might eventually come around. (The Message) –Titus 2:6-8

At the beginning of the summer in 2005, Deron assigned a couple of boys to work with me that were getting into trouble at home and at school. I had to supervise them for the entire summer. Everyday for the first week, he kept sending more boys to me and by the end of the week I ended up with fourteen boys.

Another one of my coworkers and I were responsible for them, but the brunt of the work fell on me. The age ranges of the boys were from twelve to nineteen years old. In the beginning most of them were lazy and undisciplined.

We had boys from every background; wanna be thugs and players, thieves, mama's boys, trouble makers, and even one of them was struggling with homosexuality. I had my hands full yet again. Deron called the group the *"God Sons"* and he instructed me to take them through several leadership trainings and assign them work to do throughout the day. It was hell in the beginning but after a while, they started to turn around.

One day the boys were outside at our food truck trying to get some food from the cooks and I told them to come back in the building. The ring leader of the group ignored me so I grabbed him by the arm and said, "Let's go." He snatched away and balled up his fist and said, "What you trying to do?" He was just playing but he really thought that he could take me because he was about my size.

They played this game called *"going to the body,"* where you punch each other as hard as you can until somebody quits, and he called me out. So, me being a minister I decided to apply the Scripture, Acts 6:6 and I laid hands on him. After I ministered to him for a while through the laying on of the hands he fell down and said that he quit. Then I turned around to the rest of them and asked who was next. They all shook their heads and went back into the building. We didn't have anymore problems like that after that incident.

Hey! These may not be proper Christian methods, but they worked for me. Before you can lead black, "at-risk" youth you have to first earn their respect and most of these kids were from the hood, so I had to speak their language.

After the first two weeks, I really began to bond with the boys and they began to seek me out for advice. It wasn't hard to begin to develop relationships with them because all I had to do was think about what I wanted at their age, which was somebody to care about me and spend time with me. So that is what I did. I went to their football games, took them out for their birthdays, and pretty much did things with them that a father would do.

The real problem with most of them was that their fathers were not in their lives. That is why they were rebelling because they were angry. I even recruited a couple of other men to help me with the boys outside of work hours. Eventually we had enough men working with them that I wasn't getting burnt out.

To this day, most of the boys are doing well and only a few of them ended up heading down the wrong path. However, I believe that the ones that strayed will be back because the seed of God was planted in them.

In the end, they were just as much of a blessing to me as I was to them because before I started working with them, I had planned on quitting. However, working with them gave me a purpose.

ATL Project

[21] *"Furthermore, you shall select out of all the people able men who fear God, men of truth, those who hate dishonest gain; and you shall place these over them as leaders of thousands, of hundreds, of fifties and of tens. (NASB)* **–Exodus 18:21**

[1] *To every thing there is a season, and a time to every purpose under the heaven:...* [3] *a time to break down, and a time to build up;* **–Ecclesiastes 3:1, 3b**

Our church had been traveling back and forth to Atlanta, Georgia performing one of our productions that Deron wrote entitled, *"The Boyfriend Girlfriend Thang"* and we were getting rave reviews. This eventually led to the leadership deciding to open up a satellite church in Atlanta in the summer of 2006. I was the one commissioned to head down to Atlanta with a friend of mine to oversee the construction of the church.

This is where my engineering background came in handy because I had to help prepare the blueprints for the church and the budget for all of the materials and labor cost. We worked twelve to fourteen hour days, six days a week, for three and a half months. During that process, Deron would call me from Maryland giving me instructions over the phone and I had to visit the county inspections office several times a week to expedite the inspection process so that we could get our permits.

Everyday, my colleague and I had to supervise the laborers and press the subcontractors because they were moving too slow. I would constantly get calls from Deron telling me that we needed to have the building finished yesterday.

When we finally got the occupancy permit, I laid flat on my back on the stage that we built and went to sleep for a couple of hours. I was exhausted but I was proud of myself because Deron had entrusted me to supervise the construction of the new church by myself while he stayed in Maryland to conduct services.

2008 Leadership Retreat

[35]*Cast not away therefore your* **confidence***, which hath great recompense of reward.* [36]*For ye have need of patience, that, after ye have done the will of God, ye might receive the promise.* [37]*For yet a little while, and he that shall come will come, and will not tarry.* [38]*Now the just shall live by faith: but if any man draw back, my soul shall have no pleasure in him.* [39]*But we are not of them who draw back unto perdition; but of them that believe to the saving of the soul.* *–Hebrews 10:35-39*

It is customary for us to kick off the New Year with a leadership retreat and in 2008 Deron told me that he wanted me to help him teach a segment at the retreat on *"Confidence."* I had no idea why he picked me and I was scared to death because I still suffered from stage fright due to the fact that I stuttered.

I didn't even know what I was going to talk about until I read this book by Barbara De Angelis, entitled, *"Confidence: Finding and Living It."* Below is a quote from the book that helped me to prepare my presentation:

"True confidence doesn't come from eliminating your fear. It comes from trusting yourself to act in spite of your fear." (41)

After reading the book, I realized that confidence only comes when you face your fears. So I decided to face one of my biggest fears and I went to the pet store and bought a rat. I didn't just buy any rat, but I bought the biggest rat that they had in the store. He was so big that his tale looked like a snake. No disrespect to Shaquille O'Neal, but I named the rat "Shaq".

When I first bought him, I was too scared to pick him up so a friend of mine handled Shaq for me. I then had them video tape me picking up the rat and it took me close to ten minutes before I finally picked him up. As I held him in my hand, I was shaking and then he nibbled on my finger and I threw him back in the cage and ran away screaming like a woman.

On the day of the retreat when my segment came up, I took the stage and informed the people that my topic of discussion was *"Confidence."* I recited the quote above to emphasize what true confidence is then I began to tell them how I have been terrified of rats all of my life. Then I played the video of me picking up the rat. Everybody was laughing but they got the message.

Then, I began to take some questions from the audience but I ended up excusing myself for a minute and went behind the curtain and when I came back out I had Shaq in my hand. Everybody started clapping. Later on that night, several people who were scared of rats conquered their fear and picked Shaq up as well. Shaq, the rat, became the star of the retreat.

2008 Junkyard Kids Summer Camp

[28]*Take heed therefore unto yourselves, and to all the flock, over the which the Holy Ghost hath made you overseers, to feed the church of God, which he hath purchased with his own blood.* –**Acts 20:28**

Deron has been in full-time ministry for over twenty years and he began his ministry by conducting summer camps. In 2007, Deron wrote a production called, *"Junkyard Kids"* that showcased kids in our church and in the community who could act, sing, and dance.

In 2008, Deron transformed this production into a seven-week creative arts summer camp, where the kids were trained in acting, singing, and dancing; which in turn, prepared them to perform the *"Junkyard Kids"* production live for their family and friends at the end of camp. Along with training the kids in the field of theatrical arts, we also developed a curriculum that taught them Christian values and standards.

Well, when it came time to organize the summer camp, Deron chose me to be the director. I worked as a teacher and head counselor in the summer camps before but I had never been responsible for running the entire camp.

The assistant director and I worked around the clock for three months preparing for the camp. We recruited a staff of twelve adult full-time workers and eight youth counselors. I was responsible for training, instructing, and coaching the entire staff on a daily basis. We had a pretty good staff and we never had any major problems.

There were over one hundred kids that attended the camp and I, being the director, was ultimately responsible for their safety and well-being on a daily basis. I was responsible for developing the curriculum, scheduling the events, overseeing the budget, and delegating assignments to the workers. It was like running a business. The only thing that I didn't do was conduct rehearsals for the production and run the actual show at the end of camp. Hallelujah, Praise the LORD!

At the end of the camp, the kids put on a great show and the staff was beat. Deron shared with me that this was the best camp in the history of the church. One of the main reasons why he said that was due to the fact that he barely had to get involved because I had matured to the point where he could trust me to run the camp by myself. I took a week off after that and cut my phone off. I didn't want to be bothered by anyone. I was off the grid.

2009 Man-Up Adventure Weekend

[13]*Be on the alert, stand firm in the faith, act like men, be strong. (NASB) –1 Corinthians 16:13*

Due to the fallen economy and the increased unemployment rate in the country, many of the men in our church and in the community-at-large became discouraged and began to lose hope. Deron sought to restore faith and courage in the men, so we decided for our annual men's retreat to take the men whitewater rafting. We wanted to do something challenging that would inspire the men to venture outside of their comfort zones and do something new.

I was assigned the responsibility of planning and organizing the entire trip from negotiating the trip costs, to negotiating the transportation cost, overseeing the registration process, scheduling the events, assigning the men to different groups, and coordinating the meals. I assembled a group of men and delegated some of the responsibilities to them. Over one hundred and fifty black men signed up to go whitewater rafting. Just getting them to conquer their fears and register to attend the trip was a feat within itself.

On the day we arrived, we had some minor complications but God worked everything out. Most of the men were scared to death when we boarded the rafts to go on the river, including myself. But once we got out on the water and hit the first wave we calmed down. We had a great time and there was even a point where we climbed this twenty foot rock and jumped into the river.

I had also worked it out for the men to go horseback riding and spend half of the day on the paintball field. Normally when we have events like this, many of the men don't get a chance to really enjoy themselves because they end up working. But, I planned this event so nobody would have to work and we could all participate in the activities. I was told afterward by Deron and several of the men that this was the best *"Man-Up"* retreat that we ever had. The men left rejuvenated and ready to take on the world. Of course at the end of the event, I was exhausted and when I got home I passed out.

TRUTH

1. My plans don't matter if they are not God's plans.
2. Before God will elevate you, He first has to humble you by having you serve others.
3. Growth only comes when you can accept corrections and rebukes and make the necessary adjustments.
4. The way to connect with "at-risk" youth is to give them what you wanted growing up. For me it was companionship and fatherly advice.

5. The more discipline and obedience I display, the more God can entrust to me.
6. True confidence is acting in spite of your fears.
7. God used the summer camp to teach me how to run a business and shepherd His flock.
8. The only way to lead and inspire men is to challenge them to conquer their fears but first you have to conquer your own.

16

Therapy: Get Your Mind Right

Romans 12:2 – ²And be not conformed to this world: but be ye transformed by the renewing of your mind, that ye may prove what is that good, and acceptable, and perfect, will of God.

Early on when I first began to work for the church, Deron and I had a run in. I dropped the ball on an assignment and he grabbed me and told me to stop being passive. I thought that he was playing but then he grabbed me again by both of my arms and shook me and said, "Stop being passive and move when you are supposed to move."

After that incident, I got pissed off with him for putting his hands on me. So, the next day I planned on confronting him about it. When I got to work, we had a staff meeting and Deron began to address some issues that he had with the staff. He brought up the incident with me and after he shared, it calmed me down a little bit but I still needed to talk to him about it and share my concerns.

After the staff meeting, I told him that I didn't appreciate him putting his hands on me and that it appeared to me that he did it out of anger. I also said that if my mistakes are irritating him to the point where he feels that he can't control his temper and he needs to resort to getting physical then this is not the job for me because I won't allow anyone to put their hands on me.

I told him that my own father doesn't even put his hands on me. He assured me that he didn't do it out of anger and that he was just trying to get my attention because I was not focused. After we spoke, I said I understood but in the future please, don't put your hands on me anymore.

Later on that same day, he met with me again and informed me that when we spoke earlier, my bottom lip was shaking. One of the assistant pastor's, Rivion, was there as well and they both informed me that my lip trembling while I was talking was a sign of anger.

I responded by saying that I didn't have an anger problem because I hadn't been in a physical confrontation with anyone in years. They said that just because I'm not violent anymore doesn't mean that I'm not angry and that I have learned to suppress my anger, which is why my lip was trembling.

Rivion shared that that was the same thing that used to happen to him because he had so much pent up rage that when he tried to talk, his lip would tremble. Deron always stressed that we all should get counseling but I never went. He told me that he wanted me to go because it was obvious that I had some hurt and pain buried deep in my soul.

As a result of that incident, I have been to several therapists seeking healing for my emotional wounds. In one way or another, each therapist has given me a tool that has helped me face the traumatic events that I have experienced in my life that were causing me to feel unfulfilled and worthless. Some of our wounds are so deep that they will only be healed through therapy.

Therapist No. 1

[5]Counsel in the heart of man is like deep water; but a man of understanding will draw it out. —Proverbs 20:5

The very first therapist I went to was a Christian therapist but I only met with her for one session because my schedule was too hectic and I kept missing my appointments. I don't even remember what we talked about in that session but she gave me a workbook entitled, *"Gems In The Coal Bin,"* by Arlene Hendricks.

I put the book on the shelf and didn't actually complete the book until a couple of months later when all hell was breaking loose in my life. There was one line in the book that truly spoke to me and made me realize that I really needed to get some help. In the workbook, Arlene Hendricks states:

> *"If the events of our past shape our life in the present, then we are paralyzed, trapped by circumstances over which we had no control. One of the most powerful insights into God's purpose comes from understanding that God can set us free thoroughly and completely from the influence of our past." (17)*

After reading that statement, I understood that if I wanted to be free from my fears then I was going to have to seek God for understanding or else stay trapped forever. Only God could truly heal me but He was only going to do it if I was willing to humble myself and do the work. That work was to go back and finish counseling.

Therapist No. 2

²¹Fathers, provoke not your children to anger, lest they be discouraged. **–Colossians 3:21**

I signed up, again, a year later for counseling and met with a middle-age white male therapist. When he asked me why did I sign up for counseling, I told him that I had anger problems and that I was also out of touch with my emotions, which caused me to be unable to develop any long lasting feelings for any of the women I dated in the past.

He seemed rather distant during our conversation but he had pretty good insight. When I told him my family history, he focused more on my dad and drew a road map of my dad's life based on the information that I gave him. What he concluded was that my dad had a problem with commitment and that is why I have a hard time committing myself to relationships as well.

He also said that because my father was verbally and sometimes physically abusive to me, I developed a lack of respect for authority. This is why I constantly rebelled, whenever people were correcting and rebuking me.

I also shared with him some of the challenges that I was having in ministry regarding my relationship with Deron. I didn't go into much detail but I shared with him that Deron could be very demanding and forceful at times.

The therapist then drew a parallel between Deron and my father and explained to me that both of them have similar personalities and I had some resentment against my father for how he criticized me growing up and that I was carrying that same resentment over into my relationship with Deron.

The therapist also asked me if Deron praised and recognized me with the same energy and frequency as he did when he was correcting me. I said, "Not really." He then said, "Well, if you want to overcome this area in your life then you are going to have to confront your father and Deron and begin to set some boundaries for your relationships."

I told the therapist that Deron is my coach and that it was his job to push me to be the best that I could be. The therapist said that's true but a good coach also encourages his players as well and right now you need encouragement. I ended up seeing this particular counselor four more times but then my schedule got really hectic again and I stopped going.

Tag Team Therapy

[22] For I delight in the law of God after the inward man: [23] But I see another law in my members, warring against the law of my mind, and bringing me into captivity to the law of sin which is in my members. —Romans 7:22-23

Despite the accomplishments that I achieved while working in ministry, I still felt unfulfilled. Although I was working for God, I began to neglect my personal relationship with Him and found myself focusing more on my finances and my own personal struggles; namely stuttering.

We had hit a rough patch in the ministry in 2006 with the opening of the satellite church in Atlanta and the declining economy; which resulted in the church staff receiving half-pay. A few times, things got so tight that we didn't get paid at all. That is the lot for a person working in the non-profit sector.

I began to contemplate resigning from ministry and pursuing real estate and engineering again to supplement my income. I was severely stressed out so I began to attend another round of counseling, hoping to get some clarity.

At this particular counseling center, I ended up being treated by two therapists; a white male and a white female. They were both graduate students studying to get their doctorate degrees so I felt like a lab rat.

As I began to share with them my past, which is always the first thing you do when you attend counseling, I noticed the horrific faces that the white female therapist was making. After I finished, they informed me that they had never heard of anyone who had experienced so many traumatic events in their life as I had. Whenever I would tell them something that happened to me they would say, "What did you do with your feelings and emotions?" and I would respond, "Nothing. I just went on with life as usual."

After meeting with them and witnessing their responses to the stories that I told them, I realized how horrendous my life had been. They hadn't experienced, seen, or been exposed to half of the stuff I had been through. Whenever I went to counseling and looked into their eyes, I could see that they were staring at me in amazement because they couldn't understand how someone could have been through all of what I'd been through without becoming crazy or insane.

One of the issues that I told them that I was struggling with, was my inability to relax and just enjoy life. I told them that I was always stressed out and restless. I was constantly on-guard and hadn't been able to lie down and have a peaceful night's sleep in years. At night, I wake up every hour on the hour.

Their response was that because I spent most of my life fighting, I was like a Vietnam veteran who had returned home from the war but was unable to re-adjust to civilian life. They said that I have to realize that I was no longer in those same situations that threatened my life and that I was in safe country.

Finally, they said that the war I experienced growing up was over but I was still at war in my mind and that I had to let the past go. I knew what they were saying was correct but I thought to myself, *"Easier said than done."*

The Oracle

*[8]Finally, brethren, whatever is true, whatever is honorable, whatever is right, whatever is pure, whatever is lovely, whatever is of good repute, if there is any excellence and if anything worthy of praise, dwell on these things. (NASB) –**Philippians 4:8***

[28]And we know that all things work together for good to them that love God, to them who are the called according to his purpose. –***Romans 8:28***

In 2009 I got engaged, so my fiancé and I signed up for pre-marital counseling with a Christian therapist named Dr. Betty. This was the first black therapist I had been to for counseling. Dr. Betty was real cool and down to earth. She was also a straight shooter and didn't beat around the bush; which was cool with me because she got paid by the hour and I wanted to get my monies worth.

At the end of our first session, I asked Dr. Betty what her success rate was as far as people getting married who came to see her for pre-marital counseling. She informed me that none of the couples that came to her so far for pre-marital counseling had gotten married. She also said that it didn't mean that the counseling was unsuccessful because people come to pre-marital counseling with hopes of getting married but then discover that they are not ready because they have personal issues that they have to work through before they can commit to a marriage.

Well, my engagement followed the same path as those previous couples who met with Dr. Betty and after five months of pre-marital counseling, I had concluded that my fiancé and I were not meant for each other and I called my engagement off.

I continued to see Dr. Betty for individual therapy. One of the things that she discerned about me was that I had a very pessimistic view on life and that I didn't have any real hopes for the future. I constantly focused on what was going wrong in my life instead of what was going right. She gave me several assignments to help me change my way of thinking so I could begin to focus on the good in life as opposed to the bad.

Deron always taught that most black people were traumatized and one day he said one of the men that he was training had written down the names of all of the people he knew that had died or had been killed and when he finished he had written down a total number of thirty-five names.

When I heard this, it prompted me to go home and write down every traumatic event that I could remember since the time I was born. When I finished writing all the things I could remember, I ended up with thirteen pages worth of traumatic events that I experienced.

I let Dr. Betty read what I wrote and she said that she had never seen anyone in her office that had experienced that much trauma before. She also said that writing it all down was a great start to my recovery but what I needed to do now is go back and write down everything good that came out of each one of those events.

I responded by saying that nothing good came out of any of that stuff and she said that God wouldn't allow you to go through something if He didn't plan on blessing you in the process. Therefore, I needed to pray to Him and ask Him to show me the blessings.

Dr. Betty told me that I was not only harboring a lot of anger towards my father and other people who had hurt me, but the main person that I was upset with was God. She said that I had to forgive God and going back and writing down the good that came out of my trauma would help to transform my mind and see God in a different light. I told her, "Cool" and that I would do it because I didn't have anything to lose.

TRUTH

1. Just because I am no longer violent, doesn't mean that I don't struggle with anger. Suppressed anger is just a damaging and dangerous as expressed anger.
2. In order to be free from my fears, I will have to confront my past.
3. Healing begins with confronting my father.
4. In order to have peace in my life, I must conquer the war in my mind.
5. Something good has come out of every bad situation that you have experienced but you have to pray and ask God to show you what that good thing was.

4th Quarter:

The Blessings and Purpose of Trauma

17

Our Fathers

Matthew 6:7-9 – *[7]But when ye pray, use not vain repetitions, as the heathen do: for they think that they shall be heard for their much speaking. [8]Be not ye therefore like unto them: for your Father knoweth what things ye have need of, before ye ask him. [9]After this manner therefore pray ye: Our Father which art in heaven, Hallowed be thy name.*

John 3:12 – *[12]If I have told you earthly things, and ye believe not, how shall ye believe, if I tell you of heavenly things?*

1 Corinthians 15:46 – *[46]However, the spiritual is not first, but the natural; then the spiritual. (NASB)*

After meeting with Dr. Betty, I realized that she was right. I was upset with God. Deron told me this same truth before, but I was scared to admit it. I thought that if I really expressed to God how I felt, He would strike me down. But, I later came to understand that God is merciful and He understood why I was distant from Him and through prayer and studying His Word, He revealed to me why I was reluctant to draw close to Him.

The natural precedes the supernatural. If you can't comprehend earthly things then you won't be able to comprehend heavenly things. I couldn't draw close to my Heavenly Father because I didn't have a relationship with my earthly father.

Due to my father's bad temper and violent outbursts, I began to resent him and in doing so I resented God. I saw God the same way that I saw my father, as; a tyrant, a dictator, abusive, critical, someone who was ready to beat me when I stepped out of line.

The only way I was going to break that stronghold in my mind was to make amends with my father. Therefore, I went to my dad and confronted him. I explained to him how his verbal and physical assaults traumatized me as a child. Thus resulting in my inability to express my emotions and relate to people, even God.

It wasn't easy but he listened and then he explained to me that he just didn't know how to discipline me and at the same time show affection because that was how his father raised him. He told me that his father left his mother and he had to take his father's place as head of the house. Even though he was the second oldest son, he was the most responsible, so his mother depended on him to help her take care of the family.

My father even shared with me that when he got married to his first wife, (which was before I was born) he went to visit his father in Annapolis, MD. He took his wife and his new-born son with him and when he arrived at his father's job, his father asked him why he kept coming to see him. His father told him that he didn't need him and he wanted him to go back to his mother and to stop coming to see him. Then his father went back to work.

After his father told him that, he started crying and then he got so mad that he wanted to kill his father. After a few minutes had passed, his father came back outside and apologized to him but it was too late because his heart had already been severely wounded. My father told me that from that moment on he had made up his mind not to feel and he has been like that ever since.

After he told me that story, I finally understood why he was so angry and acted the way he did. I realized that he was traumatized as well and that is when I forgave him. He was doing the best he knew how to do. He didn't realize that in choosing not to feel he was actually still feeling. His pain and grief was still being felt but it was just being expressed in the form of anger. I also realized that he needed to forgive his father as well so that he could be free.

Sins of the Fathers

*[18]'The LORD is slow to anger and abundant in lovingkindness, forgiving iniquity and transgression; but He will by no means clear the guilty, visiting the iniquity of the fathers on the children to the third and the fourth generations.' (NASB) –**Numbers 14:18***

My dad and I had several conversations regarding our relationship and as a result, we have grown a lot closer as father and son. However, I still had work to do because I inherited my father's anger and inability to express my emotions in a proper way. This required me to read several books on anger and continue to go to therapy and learn how to process how I felt before I responded to someone as opposed to just reacting.

I learned that anger is neither bad nor good but it is just an emotion and what I do with my anger is the determining factor. Anger is really passion and I had to learn how to channel that passion into something constructive versus destructive.

I no longer wear my heart on my sleeve and I have learned that it is okay to agree to disagree with people without going ballistic. Through the power of God that curse in my family line stops with me and it will not be passed on to my kids.

A Father's Discipline

[11] My son, despise not the chastening of the LORD; neither be weary of his correction: [12] For whom the LORD loveth he correcteth; even as a father the son in whom he delighteth. –Proverbs 3:11-12

[7] It is for discipline that you endure; God deals with you as with sons; for what son is there whom his father does not discipline? [8] But if you are without discipline, of which all have become partakers, then you are illegitimate children and not sons. [9] Furthermore, we had earthly fathers to discipline us, and we respected them; shall we not much rather be subject to the Father of spirits, and live? [10] For they disciplined us for a short time as seemed best to them, but He disciplines us for our good, so that we may share His holiness. (NASB) –Hebrews 12:7-10

Due to my father's unbalanced methods of raising me regarding his excessive discipline and lack of emotional support, I learned to hate and despise all discipline. Once I confronted my dad, I learned how to see the love in discipline and accept corrections and rebukes from authority figures.

Deron also shared on several occasions, how his father verbally and physically abused him and later in his life, he adopted his father's bad habits and treated people he was training the same way that his father had treated him. He also confronted and forgave his father and has since apologized to people that he mistreated. Deron has always said, "He was not qualified," and he was also doing the best he knew how to do as well because nobody trained him on how to be a father or a pastor.

Deron and I have had several conversations that have brought healing to our relationship. One time, I shared with him that I felt like he was harder on me than he was on everybody else and that he never cut me any slack.

He told me that was true and the reason why he was so hard on me was God has a special purpose for me and there was a whole lot more expected out of me than was expected out of everyone else. He told me to stop viewing his discipline as punishment, but to view it as love because he loved me like a son. He asked, "What father wouldn't want the best for his son."

The Power of a Father

21For just as the Father raises the dead and gives them life, even so the Son also gives life to whom He wishes. (NASB) **–John 5:21**

63It is the Spirit who gives life; the flesh profits nothing; the words that I have spoken to you are spirit and are life. (NASB)
–John 6:63

Shortly after my mother passed I obtained my real estate license for the state of Maryland and then I began to study to obtain my real estate license for the District of Columbia (DC). I only had to take the real estate law portion of the exam for DC since I already had my real estate license in Maryland.

I was extremely nervous as I prepared for the exam because the DC law portion of the real estate exam was a little more complicated than the Maryland law portion of the exam. After many nights of studying for the exam I finally braved the waters and took the exam and all praise be to God, I passed it.

Normally after I accomplished something like this I would call my mother and tell her but she was gone. So, I decided to call my dad. When I told him that I passed the exam he said:

> *"Terrence that's great. You were stressing out over the exam but I wasn't worried at all. I knew that you were going to pass it because you are extremely intelligent. I*

believe in you and I also believe that you can accomplish anything you put your mind to. I'm proud of you son."

I responded by saying thanks. Once we got off the phone I had to pull my car off the road because I burst into tears and began to cry uncontrollably. I didn't understand where that sudden rush of emotions came from. It was like a dam of water had burst. I realized that was what I had wanted to hear all my life, my father saying that he was proud of me. I was twenty-six years old when this occurred but I was crying like I was six years old.

Words give life, especially the affirming words of a father. My father's words released a power in me that I didn't realize I had. They helped me to believe in myself. I later used this same principle while I was working with the God Son's.

Most of them are grown men now but some of them still call me from time-to-time informing me about their achievements. I always respond by telling them that I'm proud of them and that they can accomplish anything that they put their mind to. I also tell them that they are special and that I love them. Many of them have never heard a man say that they love them. That's why I say words to encourage them because I realize they need to hear it, like I needed to hear those words from my pops.

Blessings in the Trauma

After mending my relationship with my dad and Deron, I was able to begin to see God in a different light. I realized that God has been protecting and providing for me all of my life even when I didn't want anything to do with Him. As I look back over my life through the lenses of God's Spirit and reflect on the events that transpired between my dad and I, I was able to see the blessings that came out of that chaos.

Gone to Church

When my father left me in the house at two years old to take my mother to church, I woke up scared to death. However, when I look back on it, I realize that God kept me safe. What two-year old could be home alone without seriously injuring themselves?

When my father came through the door, I jumped off of my horse, ran and jumped into his arms because I knew that I was safe. My father told me that it broke his heart to see me scared like that and he made a vow never to leave me again. Since then, he has never left me even when I got older and kept getting into trouble and God has never left me either.

The Big Bad Wolf

I don't know what prompted my parents to start fighting that day but when I walked downstairs and saw my father choking my mother, I was so horrified that I froze. Although that was a terrible thing for a four-year old to witness, God sent me downstairs because when my father saw me he came to his senses and let my mother go. Had I not walked downstairs, he possibly may have killed her. That was the last time I ever saw my parents have a physical altercation.

My First Companion, Major

The day Major chewed up my father's boat he went overboard and beat him so bad that he left a permanent knot on his head. Later on, he redeemed himself by spending over seven hundred dollars in veterinarian bills to help Major overcome heartworm disease. When Major died, that was the first time I saw my dad cry and that is when I realized that it was okay for a man to cry.

Three years after Major died, my father bought me a Rottweiler that I named Zeus. We took Zeus to the veterinarian on a consistent basis and he never got sick. Before my father bought Zeus for me, he told me that he would never get another dog and not properly take care of him. My dad always learned from his mistakes and in the end he would always do the right thing.

The Car is Fine

After my mother crashed the car, my father didn't really show much concern for our well being. But now as I reflect on that incident, I realize that for him to not go off and start yelling and screaming was an act of God because back then, my father's temper was unmanageable. So in reality, my father not saying anything was concern because if he would have said something; it probably would have been negative.

That was the only car that we had at the time, so when we had to put the car in the shop, my father had to walk to work. He would never let anything stop him from going to work. One time, he walked to work and back in the snow.

My father has a ridiculous work ethic and wherever he was employed, he ended up in some type of management position. That is where I get my work ethic from. I am the same way. That is how I could press through the engineering program at UMCP and work so hard in the ministry. My father modeled hard work and dedication and it rubbed off on me.

Science Fair Project

Although my father didn't have the patience to take his time to teach and instruct me, at least he took the time to help me with my project. I can say this now because a lot of my friends didn't have their fathers in their lives and the ones who did have fathers barely took the time to help them with their school work at all.

One thing I learned from this incident is; no matter what's on my schedule, I pray that I will always make time for my kids and give them my undivided attention because that plays a major role in building their self-esteem and confidence.

Predator

My father grew up on the mean streets of Baltimore, Maryland so he had to do a lot of fighting just to survive. Unfortunately, he brought that same street mentality into his home, which caused him to verbally and physically abuse his family at times. On the street you have to carry yourself in such a way that people will be too scared to bother you. My father carried that same philosophy over into our house which was, he wanted everybody in the house to be scared of him. He ruled our house with fear, which kept him in control.

All of my father's children were scared of him; including me. I have a total of eight brothers and two sisters and I'm second to the youngest. None of my brothers ever stood up to my father until they were grown men and became bigger and stronger than he was. However, I stood up to him to defend my mother and my little brother when I was still a boy and had no chance of beating him.

I'm not proud of attempting to fight my dad, but I am proud of the fact that I stood up to him. Out of all of the fear that I faced at school and in my neighborhood, the biggest fear that I faced on a daily basis was at home, namely my father. After standing up to him, it gave me the courage to stand up to anybody. I've learned that God can bring good out of any situation and I believe that He used the rage inside my dad to bring the warrior out of me.

You Have Fun

*[24]He who withholds his rod (discipline) hates his son, But he who loves him disciplines him diligently. (NASB) – **Proverbs 13:24***

If God ever blesses me to have children, prayerfully I will not discipline them like my father disciplined me at times. But, I am thankful for my father because it was the fear that I had for my dad that kept me out of a lot of trouble.

As I stated earlier, many of my friends' fathers were not involved in their lives or their fathers were passive and weak; which allowed them to grow up without any discipline. They ran the streets all day and night, but my father wasn't having that.

He was strict at times but his strictness is what kept me out of trouble. Today, I know of a lot of people who have died, are in jail, have too many kids that they can't support and who work dead end jobs because growing up they didn't have a father to instill any discipline in their lives.

I thank God for my dad, even though he was a little rough around the edges. Because of my dad's discipline, I was able to avoid many of the pitfalls that took many of my friends out and caused them not to reach their fullest potential in life.

Go Ahead and Kill Me

*[4]And, ye fathers, provoke not your children to wrath: but bring them up in the nurture and admonition of the Lord. –**Ephesians 6:4***

If I could do it all over again, I would never have fought my father because I have learned that to dishonor your parents is a violation of God's law. However, I believe that God had grace on me because He knew that my actions were provoked by my dad's bad temper.

The one good thing that came out of this incident when my dad was choking me was it made him look into the mirror at himself and realize that his anger was destroying our family.

The more he tried to control and intimidate me, the angrier I became. I had turned into him. Matthew 12:26 states, *"Satan can't cast out Satan,"* and I believe that my father understood that in order for me to change, he was going to have to change first. Anger can't cast out anger. Only love can do that.

Give God A Shot

When God saves a man, He saves the man's whole family because the man is designated by God to be the leader of his household. When a real man gets saved, he leads his whole family to God. When my father gave his life to Christ that also lead me to eventually give my life to Christ as well. My father gave God a shot and God didn't let him down. As a result my father has been serving in his church ever since and so have I.

I Look Like A Monster

[8]Better is the end of a thing than the beginning –Ecclesiastes 7:8a

Ever since I was a little boy, my parent's marriage was unstable. From time-to-time my mother entertained the thoughts of getting a divorce. However, divorce was not in God's plan for my parents. In fact, he used my mother's illness to bring them closer together.

I remember when my mother had those panic attacks, screaming and saying "What is God doing to me? I look like a monster!" because her face had swollen so much where she couldn't distinguish her nose from her face. During her panic attacks my father would hold her and tell her that she was still beautiful. God transformed my dad from being mean, insensitive and violent to a caring, compassionate and loving husband and father.

He truly honored his wedding vows and hung in there with my mother through "better and for worse" and "sickness and in health," until death did them apart. If it is God's will for me to get married and my wife ends up getting sick, I pray to God that I will be half the man that my father was. I'm proud of my pops. He is a true CHAMPION.

TRUTH

1. If you haven't made amends with your earthly father then it will be difficult to relate to your Heavenly Father.
2. The sins of my father were passed on to me, but I must do the work so that the curse in my family line (namely anger) stops with me.
3. When God continues to send trials my way, it's evidence of His love for me because He disciplines those He loves.
4. I get my tenacious work ethic from my father who never missed work and was promoted to supervisory positions wherever he was employed.
5. God used the anger and rage in my dad to bring out the warrior in me.
6. God used my dad's dedication and care for my mother during her illness as a model of what a true husband is supposed to be, so whenever God sends me a wife, I will have a road map to follow.

-18-

Wheat and Weeds

Matthew 13:24-30 —*[24]Jesus presented another parable to them, saying, "The kingdom of heaven may be compared to a man who sowed good seed in his field. [25]"But while his men were sleeping, his enemy came and sowed tares (noxious weeds) among the wheat, and went away. [26]"But when the wheat sprouted and bore grain, then the tares became evident also. [27]"The slaves of the landowner came and said to him, 'Sir, did you not sow good seed in your field? How then does it have tares?' [28]"And he said to them, 'An enemy has done this!' The slaves said to him, 'Do you want us, then, to go and gather them up?' [29]"But he said, 'No; for while you are gathering up the tares, you may uproot the wheat with them. [30]'Allow both to grow together until the harvest; and in the time of the harvest I will say to the reapers, "First gather up the tares and bind them in bundles to burn them up; but gather the wheat into my barn."'" (NASB)*

As I look back over my life I realized that God has spared me on several occasions. I often wondered why God extended so much grace to me, especially when I had made up my mind to live in total opposition to His will. One of the reasons why God spared my life was due to the prayers of my mother and her constant pleading with God on my behalf.

Later on, I found out that while she was taking chemotherapy and going through her radiation treatments she would still fast for me and not eat any food because she knew that I was headed down the wrong path and only God could step in and save me. God honored her request and never allowed me to truly suffer the consequences that my sins deserved namely; prison, a sexually transmitted disease, children out of wedlock, and even death.

Another reason why God spared me was He knew the true motives of my heart. Deep down inside I was a good person but I just didn't have any spiritual guidance. It wasn't until my father got saved that I really began to examine myself and see the error of my ways. God is patient and He always gives people ample time to change and turn to Him for salvation.

When I first started reading the Bible, one of the Scripture passages that caught my attention was Matthew 13:24-3, where Jesus talked about the wheat and the weeds. He explained that God didn't allow His angels to uproot the weeds because in doing so they would also mistakenly uproot the wheat; as well.

The reason for this is when wheat and weeds first begin to bud they look the same. It is not until they have fully grown up that you can distinguish one from the other.

This is why all judgment is left to God and not to man or even to the angels because only God knows what the outcome of your life is going to be. Therefore, no matter how wretched or wicked you were in the beginning of your life, there is always an opportunity to be redeemed while you're on this side of eternity.

God is a specialist in using people who have fallen short of His standards of holiness. Even in your sins, He still keeps His promise to carry out His will in your life because the gifts and call of God are irrevocable (Romans 11:29).

One of the reasons many people struggle with giving their lives to God is they believe that they are beyond being saved because of their sinful lifestyles. To help counter this mindset, I listed a few people along with their shortcomings who were major contributors in carrying out God's purpose in the earth.

1. **Moses** was a murderer and had a bad temper. (Exodus 2:11-12 & Numbers 20:2-12)
2. **Sampson** was a fornicator and slept with prostitutes. (Judges 16:1)
3. **King David** was an adulterer, a murderer and prideful. (2 Samuel 11:1-27 & 2 Samuel 24:1-25)
4. **King Solomon** disobeyed God and married pagan women and ended up worshiping their gods. (1 Kings 11:1-8)
5. **Peter** was a hot-tempered man who resorted to violence. (John 18:10-11)
6. **James & John** were so angry that Jesus nicknamed them *"Sons of Thunder."* (Mark 3:17 & Luke 9:51-56)
7. **Paul,** before his conversion, hunted Christians and had them killed. (Acts 22:2b-4)

Despite their sins, each one of the men listed above was empowered by God to do great things and ultimately fulfilled their purpose in life. The key to their restoration and triumph was their willingness to humble themselves before God and ask God for forgiveness for their sins.

Repentance is the key which unlocks the door to God's grace and redemption. No matter who you are or what you have done, turn to God and confess your sins and accept Jesus Christ as your Lord and Savior and God will forgive you and give you a new start on life. God planted you as wheat and not as a weed.

[16]For God so loved the world, that he gave his only begotten Son, that whosoever believeth in him should not perish, but have everlasting life. –John 3:16

Blessings in the Trauma

High Profile Student

[8]And there were in the same country shepherds abiding in the field, keeping watch over their flock by night. –Luke 2:8

The reason I got into so much trouble in high school was I just wanted some attention. I really wasn't a bad kid and I thank God that my administrator, Dr. Sullivan, was able to see through my façade. He noticed that I was smart and just needed the proper motivation. He was a stern man, but God placed it in his heart to look out for me and not to expel me from school. I was a lost sheep in high school but Dr. Sullivan was one of my shepherds.

Security, Security, Man Down!

[4]For the LORD your God is he that goeth with you, to fight for you against your enemies, to save you. –Deuteronomy 20:4

This incident helped me to truly see the flaws in our judicial system. I was the person who was assaulted; but because I was black in a predominantly white establishment, I was sent to jail.

When we went to court, my attorney presented a plea bargain to me that was offered by the security company's attorney. I told our attorney that I would not accept the plea bargain because I was not guilty and once the trial starts he needs to represent me and fight for my freedom because that is what he was paid to do.

I also told him that if the judge finds me guilty, then I would suffer the consequences but I was not going to bow down and accept a deal because I was the victim. I took a stand for justice and God blessed me by allowing one of the security guards to tell the truth, which ultimately led to me being found not guilty. It was only by the grace of God that a young black male was able to win a trial involving a physical confrontation with a white man in the state of Virginia. The Lord fought for me. Praise God!

This charge was expunged from my record and this incident also brought me and my father closer because he never gave up on me and he supported me through the entire process. Despite all of the trouble that I had gotten myself into he was always there to bail me out, whether I was right or wrong. Once the truth came out, my father was actually proud of me for defending myself and not taking that plea bargain.

They Shootin'

¹⁷A friend loveth at all times, and a brother is born for adversity.
–Proverbs 17:17

I regret having gone to the school to fight that night but I only went because I was looking out for my friend. I have always been a loyal person, but I learned that my loyalties were misplaced. I just thank God that no one was seriously injured that night, especially my family.

This experience caused me to become very cautious and selective in making friends. I've come to the understanding that my friendship is priceless and I will go to hell and back for a friend and I also deserve a friend like that in return. True friendship is to be earned not given.

Road Rage

I just thank God that nobody got hurt and incidents like this just proved to me, without a shadow of a doubt, that God has always kept His hand of protection on me. I was totally out of control back then but God spared me because He knew that ultimately I was a good seed that was just planted in bad soil. Once He changed the soil, which was my environment, then I would grow into the man He was calling me to be. The end of a thing is better than the beginning (Ecclesiastes 7:8a).

Look At His Face

[11b]A hurricane wind ripped through the mountains and shattered the rocks before GOD, but GOD wasn't to be found in the wind; after the wind an earthquake, but GOD wasn't in the earthquake; [12]and after the earthquake fire, but GOD wasn't in the fire; and after the fire a gentle and quiet whisper. (The Message) –1 Kings 19:11b-12

This was the first time I ever heard God speaking to me and as a result I didn't take the life of an innocent man. It wasn't an audible voice but it was a prompting in my spirit. After that, I stopped looking for the dudes who shot at my house and I put the incident behind me. I decided to let the police handle it.

Self-Destruction

[9]He (the Lord) will not always strive with us, Nor will He keep His anger forever. [10]He has not dealt with us according to our sins, Nor rewarded us according to our iniquities. (NASB) –Psalm 103:9-10

As I stated earlier, this was a period in my life where I had little-to-no spiritual guidance and as a result, I began to get totally out of control. It was only the grace of God that I didn't get locked up, get someone pregnant, contract a sexually transmitted disease or get killed. God extended a lot of grace to me during this time because He knew that He had a plan for my life. This has taught me that I need to be willing to extend this same grace to others. He who has been forgiven much loves much (Luke 7:47).

Prisoners of the State

3Remember the prisoners, as though in prison with them, and those who are ill-treated, since you yourselves also are in the body. (NASB) –Hebrews 13:3

When two of my closest friends went to jail, I was heartbroken but afterwards I began to keep to myself because I really wasn't close to the other guys who hung around us. This led me to check in and focus more on the engineering program at UMCP.

Andre had a lot of support from his family but Kevin didn't because his mother and his sister were strapped financially and all of his other friends turned their backs on him. Kevin was like my big brother and there was no way I was going to abandon him while he was in prison. So, I kept visiting him, sending him money and writing him letters for six years. He got saved while he was in prison and even became the prison's youth pastor.

This is another example of a person who looked like a weed but really was wheat. God also used this season to teach me how to go the distance with a friend in need. I don't take any credit for anything I did for Kevin while he was in prison because it was God who inspired me and gave me the resources to be a blessing to my friend.

TRUTH

1. God can save and use anybody and all judgment belongs to Him and Him alone.
2. God has a plan for everyone's life and He will see it through to completion.
3. How you start in life isn't as important as how you finish.
4. The more that God has forgiven you for, the more He requires you to love.
5. I am a loyal friend and I deserve that same type of friendship in return.

-19-

Jesus of the Hood

John 1:43-46 *– ⁴³The next day He (Jesus) purposed to go into Galilee, and He found Philip and Jesus said to him, "Follow Me." ⁴⁴Now Philip was from Bethsaida, of the city of Andrew and Peter. ⁴⁵ Philip found Nathanael and said to him, "We have found Him of whom Moses in the Law and also the Prophets wrote--Jesus of Nazareth, the son of Joseph." ⁴⁶Nathanael said to him, **"Can any good thing come out of Nazareth?"** Philip said to him, "Come and see." (NASB)*

God's ultimate desire for man is for us to have a relationship with Him. The root word for the word relationship is "relate". To relate means to have similar interest or things in common.

When I first got saved, I found it difficult to build a relationship with God because I didn't relate to God. Whenever I heard sermons about Christ, they all portrayed Him as this mild-mannered, soft spoken individual. Furthermore, every movie I saw about Jesus or any Biblical account, all starred white actors. Therefore, I was unable to draw a parallel to God.

Fortunately, through the study of God's Word, He revealed to me that I have more in common with Jesus than I thought. Jesus was from Nazareth, a little town located within the district of Galilee. Galilee, along with Nazareth, was a despised region and many of the Jewish religious leaders didn't expect the Messiah to come from such a place (John 7:45-52).

The people in Nazareth were prone to violence and even sought to kill Jesus for His testimony concerning Himself being the fulfillment of the Messianic prophecy (Luke 4:14-30). They took offense to Jesus and He was unable to do anymore miracles in His hometown, thus the saying, *"A prophet is without honor in his hometown"* (Matthew 13:53-58).

The description of Nazareth and its inhabitants is a direct correlation to my neighborhood and the neighborhoods where most of my family and friends were raised. The region was despised and looked down upon, which in turn produced a group of people who

153

were cynical and hostile. For all intents and purposes, Jesus was raised in the hood.

This revelation raised a question, *"Why would God allow His Son to be raised in such a hostile environment?"* The answer is simple, God knew the danger and opposition that Christ would face as He set out to conduct His ministry. Allowing Him to be raised in such a place would prepare Him mentally, physically and spiritually to confront any and all obstacles set before Him.

Now, I'm not saying that Jesus grew up fighting on the streets of Nazareth or that He was a gang-banger. However, growing up in that type of environment will produce fortitude and an unrelenting resolve in the spirit of an individual.

Jesus was a strong-willed and assertive man; far from passive and docile as He is typically portrayed in Hollywood. His environment, along with the Spirit of God, made Him that way. Below are some accounts of Jesus and how His indomitable Spirit propelled His ministry despite opposition from religious leaders, government officials and demonic forces.

- Jesus confronted two violent demon-possessed men who had everyone in the region scared to pass their way. He also overpowered the demons and cast them out after they begged Him not to torment them before the appointed time. (Matthew 8:28-33)
- Jesus' twelve disciples were made up of fishermen, hotheads, revolutionaries and tax collectors. A weak man can't lead and demand the respect of a group of men, especially a group of roughnecks. (Mark 3:13-19)
- Jesus said He didn't come to bring peace to the world but a sword. Meaning commitment to the Father was His first and foremost priority, even if it meant losing His life. (Matthew 10:34-39)
- Jesus forcefully rebuked the religious leaders for being hypocrites. (Matthew 15:1-14)
- Jesus ignored the threats of King Herod and called him a fox and told the Pharisees that He would continue to carry out His purpose despite their opposition. (Luke 13:31-32)
- Jesus rebuked His disciples for being fearful and not courageous enough to face a storm. (Mark 4:35-41)

- Jesus made a whip and physically threw people out of the temple for turning it into a marketplace and the chief priests became fearful of Him. (Mark 11:15-19 & John 2:12-17)
- Jesus went back to Jerusalem to raise Lazarus from the dead despite being warned by His disciples that there were people in Jerusalem who plotted to kill Him. (John 11:1-16)
- Jesus confronted the mob that came to take Him away to be crucified and they became frightened of Him because of His majesty. (John 18:1-11)
- Jesus refused to take a drug to numb Him from the pain of the cross. (Matthew 27:34)
- Jesus was able to survive on the cross for six hours after He was tortured and beaten all night prior to His crucifixion. (Mark 15:25-37)
- After His physical death, Jesus went to hell to preach and to battle for the keys to death and Hades and rose on the third day with all power. (1 Peter 3:18-22 & Revelation 1:17-18)

Jesus was the strongest, toughest, bravest, wisest, and most loved and feared man that has ever walked the face of the earth. He had more courage than any general of war and more splendor than any king or ruler that the world has ever known. He was the epitome of what a true man looks and acts like.

He had totally devoted Himself to the will of God with total disregard for His own life. He wasn't raised with a silver spoon in His mouth and He spent most of His time hanging with people who lived in the gutter (Matthew 9:9-13).

If He walked the streets today, He would be in the ghettoes healing the sick and recruiting society's outcasts: drug dealers, gang bangers, junkies, alcoholics, prostitutes, murderers, and thieves. Why? Because He Himself, was an outcast. He was from Nazareth and He was called a Nazarene (Matthew 2:19-23).

This revelation about the life of Jesus greatly inspired me and for the first time I understood why God allowed me to be raised in such a hostile environment. God knew that He would eventually call me to help spread His gospel and just like Jesus I had to be courageous enough to confront anything that opposed His will. Passive men cannot advance God's kingdom (Matthew 11:12). This is why God takes men through the wilderness to train them for spiritual warfare.

[1]These are the nations that GOD left there, using them to test the Israelites who had no experience in the Canaanite wars. [2]He did it to train the descendants of Israel, the ones who had no battle experience, in the art of war. (The Message) **–Judges 3:1-2**

Can any good thing come out of:
- o   **Nazareth?** Yes, **Jesus Christ**
- o   **Oxon Hill, Maryland?** Yes, **Terrence Jones**
- o   _____? Yes, _____
         (Your Hood)   (Your Name)

Blessings in the Trauma

Punching Bag

[7]But the LORD said unto Samuel, Look not on his countenance, or on the height of his stature; because I have refused him: for the LORD seeth not as man seeth; for man looketh on the outward appearance, but the LORD looketh on the heart. **–1 Samuel 16:7**

I was always self-conscious about my size, which led me to second guess myself. I was too scared to stand up for myself because I was so much smaller than everybody else. However, I learned a valuable lesson and that is your physical stature doesn't matter, but it is the size of your heart that counts. Everybody always looked over me because I was small and quiet but God didn't because He knew that enclosed in that small frame of mine was the heart of a lion because He put it there.

I never had anyone to take up for me which ended up being a blessing because I had to learn to fend for myself. This helped me to develop fortitude and a willingness to face my trials and not tuck tail and run from adversity. God doesn't want His people to run from opposition but towards it. The Lord's army only marches in one direction and that's forward.

Welcome to Junior High

[3]The fining pot is for silver and the furnace for gold: but the LORD trieth (tests) the hearts. **–Proverbs 17:3**

God used middle school to toughen me up because I had no choice but to stand up for myself. It was in middle school that I learned to endure constant criticism and harassment. This is where I learned that unless you stand up and defend yourself, the world will tear you apart. The more you let people push you around, then the more they will push you around. If you want respect, then you will have to earn it. So, I learned to earn it and have been earning it ever since.

Where Y'all From?

[24]Friends come and friends go, but a true friend sticks by you like family. (The Message) –Proverbs 18:24

There were six of us walking home that night, but two of the guys were not part of our crew. As a matter of fact they were the reason that we got jumped because their neighborhood beat up one of the boys whose neighborhood we were walking through. The dudes thought my friends and I were from that same neighborhood as well. I got hit first, and then everybody ran.

My friend Moe and I got beat up the worst. After they finished hitting me, I got up and saw a group of boys still hitting Moe. I didn't leave him and I told them to let him go. After they let him go, we ran. One thing I learned is never abandon your friends.

I also learned never let people hang around me if I don't know their history because they could bring unnecessary drama into my life. Again, friendship is proven over time. This principle has kept me out of a lot of trouble.

Junior High School Fights

[1]Blessed be the LORD, my Rock, Who trains my hands for war, and my fingers for battle; (NASB) –Psalm 144:1

Out of all of the fights that I had in middle school, I wasn't responsible for starting any of them but I also didn't avoid them either. I had had it with people taking advantage of me. When I look back over my seventh and eighth grade years, I realize that these were some of the worst years of my life; constant criticism, ridicule, fear, threats, and fights.

The one good thing that came out of this season in my life was that my reputation changed. People went from disrespecting me to respecting me and I also began to respect myself. This was God's plan all along, which was to get me to stand up for myself and reclaim my self-respect.

Death Threat

[4]Yea, though I walk through the valley of the shadow of death, I will fear no evil: for thou art with me; thy rod and thy staff they comfort me. —Psalm 23:4

When those older guys threatened me in my first year of high school, it was the same ole, same ole; being picked on again because I was alone and didn't have anyone to look out for me. Even though I was scared, I still went to school. Many people in my position would have skipped school until the situation blew over but I didn't. I figured they were just going to have to do whatever they felt they had to do. God had given me the courage not to run anymore.

War Zone

[11]For he shall give his angels charge over thee, to keep thee in all thy ways. —Psalm 91:11

High school was hell and there were many people who didn't live to graduate. I had a couple of close encounters with death myself. I just thank God that through it all, He had mercy on me and preserved my life. My mother always said that God had His angels watching over me.

Dead Men Walking

[4]Again he said unto me, Prophesy upon these bones, and say unto them, O ye dry bones, hear the word of the LORD. [5]Thus saith the

Lord GOD unto these bones; Behold, I will cause breath to enter into you, and ye shall live: –Ezekiel 37:4-5

Despite the numbness of my heart due to the violence I witnessed, God still breathed the breath of life into my soul. This quickening of my spirit was the result of counseling, prayer and studying God's Word, which allowed me to see how God used my circumstances to equip me with the courage to stand for Him and to prepare me for my destiny. God raises His people on the battlefields of life to train them for spiritual warfare.

TRUTH

1. Jesus was a spiritual revolutionary that single-handedly overthrew the powers of darkness. He was far from passive and weak. He was a warrior king.
2. Jesus' life was the epitome of true manhood and a model that every man should follow.
3. God uses your adverse circumstances to form you into a weapon that He will use for the purpose of advancing His kingdom.
4. God will resuscitate your soul by breathing your purpose into your spirit.

20

Piece of Bread

Proverbs 6:20-26 —[20]*My son, keep thy father's commandment, and forsake not the law of thy mother:* [21]*Bind them continually upon thine heart, and tie them about thy neck.* [22]*When thou goest, it shall lead thee; when thou sleepest, it shall keep thee; and when thou awakest, it shall talk with thee.* [23]*For the commandment is a lamp; and the law is light; and reproofs of instruction are the way of life:* [24]*To keep thee from the evil woman, from the flattery of the tongue of a strange woman.* [25]*Lust not after her beauty in thine heart; neither let her take thee with her eyelids.* [26]*For by means of a **whorish woman** a man is brought to a **piece of bread**: and the adultress will hunt for your precious life.*

Proverbs 21:17 – [17]*He who loves pleasure will become a poor man; He who loves wine and oil will not become rich. (NASB)*

Solomon was the wisest and wealthiest king to ever walk the face of the earth; but his Achilles heel was women. He disobeyed the commands of God and married pagan women and began to worship their gods (1 Kings 11:1-8). At the time of King Solomon's reign, the nation of Israel was at the pinnacle of their power but because of Solomon's sinful acts with the pagan women he married, God tore the kingdom of Israel in half; which ultimately marked the nations decline (1 Kings 11:9-13).

It would only be fitting that after Solomon was confronted by God for his transgressions that he would then instruct his son to avoid the mistakes he made regarding illicit sexual affairs. In Proverbs 6:26, Solomon warns his son to stay away from prostitutes (wayward women) because they will reduce your life to a piece of bread.

A piece of bread signifies poverty and ruin and the loss of one's destiny. This not only holds true for a man's life but it also applies to a woman as well. If a woman allows herself to engage in sexual immorality, she too will be reduced to a life of poverty and become spiritually bankrupt. Illicit sexual relations are only a momentary pleasure but the consequences of such actions can last a lifetime.

Loss of Vision

*¹⁸Where there is no vision, the people perish: —**Proverbs 29:18a***

After my mother passed away, I began to lose sight of God. Up until that point, I had abstained from sex for over three years; but I lost my focus on God and began to drift back into my old habits. Eventually, I began to have sex again in hopes of numbing the pain that I was feeling. The more pain I felt, the more sex I had with different women to medicate myself.

In the end, sex just made matters even worse because I didn't have any feelings for the women that I was sleeping with but they were getting emotionally attached to me. However, after I got my fix, I would leave them heartbroken. I ruined several relationships in the process.

By no means will I dishonor my mother by using her death as an excuse as to why I began to practice sex again; but because I didn't have a clear vision and a purpose for my life, I lowered my standards and began to gratify the desires of my flesh.

Restored Vision

*¹²Restore to me the joy of Your salvation and sustain me with a willing spirit. ¹³Then I will teach transgressors Your ways, and sinners will be converted to You. (NASB) —**Psalm 51:12-13***

*³⁰A good thrashing purges evil; punishment goes deep within us. (The Message) —**Proverbs 20:30***

*⁸For he that soweth to his flesh shall of the flesh reap corruption; but he that soweth to the Spirit shall of the Spirit reap life everlasting. —**Galatians 6:8***

A few years later when I first began to assist Deron, I confessed to him about the women I was having sex with. He was the first person to inform me that if I continued down that path, then my life would be reduced to a piece of bread.

He explained to me that the more I indulged in sex, the longer I will hinder myself from achieving my purpose in life. He also told me that if I didn't change, then I wouldn't be able to work with him; which would result in forfeiture of the training I was receiving and ultimately cause me to miss out on fulfilling my destiny. This was the motivation that I needed to make the turn and begin to practice abstinence again.

I never understood why I continued to give into my sexual desires because whenever I had sex I didn't enjoy it because of the shame and conviction that followed the act. I wanted to do what's right according to God's Word, but I ended up doing the very things that I didn't want to do because of the sin that was living in me (Romans 7:14-25).

Instead of seeking God to deliver me from my pain, I sought to deliver myself; which caused my condition to get even worse. Instead of enduring the pain that God was allowing into my life to cleanse me, I was numbing it with sex. The only thing that could help me override my desire to sin was a stronger desire to see God's purpose being fulfilled in my life.

Once I got reconnected with God's plan for my life, I then had the fortitude to walk away from my sin and stay away. Galatians 6:7b states, *"for whatsoever a man soweth, that shall he also reap,"* and I realized that if I continued to sow bad seeds, then I will continue to reap a bad harvest. The only way that I can get to where God is trying to take me is to start sowing to please the Spirit and stop sowing to please my flesh.

Gateway to Demonic Influence

*[1]The words of King Lemuel, the strong advice his mother gave him: [2]"Oh, son of mine, what can you be thinking of! Child whom I bore! The son I dedicated to God! [3]Don't dissipate your **virility** on fortune-hunting women, promiscuous women who shipwreck leaders (kings). (The Message) −Proverbs 31:1-3*

[15]Know ye not that your bodies are the members of Christ? shall I then take the members of Christ, and make them the members of an

harlot? God forbid. [16]What? know ye not that he which is joined to an harlot is one body? for two, saith he, shall be one flesh. [17]But he that is joined unto the Lord is one spirit. [18]Flee fornication. Every sin that a man doeth is without the body; but he that committeth fornication sinneth against his own body. [19]What? know ye not that your body is the temple of the Holy Ghost which is in you, which ye have of God, and ye are not your own? [20]For ye are bought with a price: therefore glorify God in your body, and in your spirit, which are God's. –1 Corinthians 6:15-20

Sexual immorality not only leads to sexually transmitted diseases and unwanted pregnancies but it also opens the door of your soul to demonic oppression. Your body is a temple that houses the Holy Spirit. When you practice sex you are defiling your temple and God's Spirit can't dwell in an unclean temple. Once God's Spirit vacates your temple, then your soul will be left unguarded; which allows demons to enter and take over.

Sex is one of the main conduits that demons use to transfer from one person to another. Contrary to popular belief, sexual intercourse is not only an act which unites people physically but it also unites them emotionally and spiritually. This is why people become heartbroken after their relationship has ended because they had become emotionally attached to the person; which is always a result of sexual intercourse.

The spiritual decline caused by sexual immorality is best depicted in the life of King Solomon. The sexual relations he had with the pagan women that he took to become his wives, eventually led him away from God. He became influenced by his wives and began to practice their religions and he committed evil in the eyes of the Lord by worshiping pagan idols, which are ultimately demons (1 Kings 11:1-10).

Furthermore, when a man ejaculates inside of a woman, he becomes exhausted because ejaculation is the process of a man releasing his semen (seed); which is also his spirit (life force). A male orgasm is more than just a good feeling, but it is the passing of his life into another.

This explains how a man can impregnate a woman and never see or interact with his child; however, the child will not only grow up to have some of their father's physical features but that child will also mimic their father's characteristics as well. This is possible because the child was created by their father's seed (spirit). This is why Jesus Christ was born sinless because He was not born by a man's corrupted seed (spirit) but He was born by the Holy Spirit of God (John 1:13).

Furthermore, in Proverbs 31:1-3, King Lemuel's mother pleaded with him to avoid sexual immorality because it would rob him of his virility; which is synonymous with words such as: vigor, power, spirit, energy, health, youth, life and strength. Many people spend years in bad relationships only to look up and realize that they wasted a lot of precious time that could have been used to carry out their dreams.

Sex was instituted by God for two express purposes: 1) for the pleasure and enjoyment between a husband and his wife, which will also assist both in resisting temptation (1 Corinthians 7:1-5) and 2) to produce life so mankind could populate the earth and subdue it (Genesis 1:26-28). God's desire for sex was to be a tool to strengthen the bond between husband and wife and to ensure the existence of mankind but the enemy has perverted sex and he uses it to destroy life and to ruin a person's destiny.

God's Grace

8The LORD is compassionate and gracious, slow to anger and abounding in lovingkindness. 9He will not always strive with us, nor will He keep His anger forever. 10He has not dealt with us according to our sins, nor rewarded us according to our iniquities. (NASB) –Psalm 103:8-10

I thank God for the grace that He has extended to me. He has never repaid me according to what my sins deserved. I have suffered consequences as a result of my sinful actions but never to the extent of the pain that I caused to others. I do realize that my sins have resulted in the postponement of my blessing because many of my prayers had been directed toward God's forgiveness for my sins rather than toward His favor to empower me to carry out my purpose.

As I reflect over my life, I can see how God allowed certain things to happen to me that He used to keep me off of the path of sin and maintain a life of purity. Despite the shame, pain and fear that I experienced as result of certain events, I now realize that God used those events to protect me.

Blessings in the Trauma

Dancing Machine

[33]The fear of the LORD is the instruction of wisdom; and before honour is humility. **–Proverbs 15:33**

After everyone laughed at me at the party, I became very insecure about approaching females and dancing in front of people. This turned out to be a good thing because it kept me from going to a lot of parties where many people I knew got stabbed, shot, and some even killed.

Incidents like this kept me in a shell, but that shell kept me safe at times. God eventually cracked that shell when I became mature enough to maintain self-control and exercise restraint regarding dating and respecting women.

Picture Imperfect

[5]At this time Adonijah, whose mother was Haggith, puffed himself up saying, "I'm the next king!" He made quite a splash, with chariots and riders and fifty men to run ahead of him. [6]His father had spoiled him rotten as a child, never once reprimanding him. Besides that, he was very good-looking and the next in line after Absalom. (The Message) **–1 Kings 1:5-6**

After taking those funny looking pictures in the seventh grade, I became ashamed of my smile and my looks. This incident humbled me because ever since I was a little boy, girls always told me that I was cute and I started to become conceited. However, once everyone, including my teacher, laughed at my pictures, I became severely self-conscious and shy and didn't have the courage to approach girls; even the ones who liked me.

Again, as pitiful as it sounds this actually turned out to work in my favor because many of my friends became sexually active at that age and many of them contracted sexually transmitted diseases and/or had several children out of wedlock that they are currently struggling to support. In retrospect, dodging females back then actually helped me dodge some fatal bullets.

Blood Drive

[27]The fear of the LORD is a fountain of life, that one may avoid the snares of death. (NASB) –Proverbs 14:27

Once I heard the news about several people in our high school that tested positive for HIV, I became very fearful about having sex. Unlike many of my friends, I abstained from sex while most of them were sleeping with as many females as they could. However, as I got older, I succumbed to peer-pressure and my own wicked desires and I began to have sex as well.

Even though it was wrong, I was very cautious and protected myself physically. However, I didn't know this then, but you may be able to protect yourself from physical diseases while having sex but you can't protect yourself from spiritual diseases, which will cause you more pain in the end.

I would advise anyone to abstain from sex because having sex is a violation of God's law and whether you catch a sexually transmitted disease or not, sex can still ruin your life and the lives of others. If I could turn back the hands of time with the knowledge that I have now I would have maintained my virginity.

What, You Leaving Me?

[18]Pride goeth before destruction, and an haughty spirit before a fall. –Proverbs 16:18

At this point in my life I had become super-conceited because I was pretty much able to pull any female that I wanted. Even though I stuttered at school or on job interviews, I never stuttered when it came to talking to women. For some reason, I developed a confidence (false confidence) in myself when it came to getting women. I felt like Goldie in the movie, *"The Mack."* I was never hurt by a woman until I got my heart broken by my ex-girlfriend.

The pain of a broken heart is one of the worse pains that a person can ever experience.

When I prayed to God to take away the pain, He said, "No," and that I was going to have to endure it. God showed me that the pain I was feeling was the same pain I had put numerous women through. After experiencing it first hand, I didn't want to cause anyone else that type of pain again.

Unlike most people who jump right back into another relationship to get over their previous relationship, I chose to give my life to God and leave women alone for a season. I chose this route because I wanted God to mend my heart so there would be no residue from any past relationships. Therefore, in the future I would be able to give my future wife my whole heart instead of just a portion of it.

TRUTH

1. Sex outside of marriage leads to a life of financial and spiritual poverty.
2. The momentary gratification of sex brings more pain into your life than relief.
3. Sex not only unites people physically, but it also unites them emotionally and spiritually.
4. Sex opens the door to demonic oppression.
5. Sex used according to God's law creates life and provides enjoyment in a marriage but the enemy uses sex to destroy your life and to ruin your destiny.
6. God never repays us according to what our sins deserve.
7. God uses the pain and shame of your circumstances to humble you and to protect you with the ultimate goal of bringing you closer to Him.

21

Principalities and Personalities

Ephesians 6:10-12 – *[10]Finally, my brethren, be strong in the Lord, and in the power of his might. [11]Put on the whole armour of God, that ye may be able to stand against the wiles of the devil. [12]For we wrestle not against flesh and blood (human beings), but against principalities (demonic forces), against powers, against the rulers of the darkness of this world, against spiritual wickedness in high places.*

One of the main reasons I had trouble giving my life to Christ was I didn't believe that God was concerned about the plight of black people. I was introduced to the struggles that black people faced at a young age by my parents and as I got older, I began to experience racism first hand for myself. I just didn't understand why God would subject my people to so much oppression.

I didn't want anything to do with God because I felt that He didn't want anything to do with my people. Even to this day we are still racially profiled, crucified in the media, have sub-standard schools due to lackluster funding, and the list goes on.

It wasn't until I began to pray to God and ask for understanding that He opened up my mind and delivered me from my warped sense of thinking. In his book, *"Beyond Roots: In Search of Blacks In The Bible"*, William Dwight McKissic, Sr. states the following:

"The Bible clearly teaches that all mankind derived from Noah and his sons (Acts 17:26, Genesis 9:18-19). Noah had three sons named Ham, Shem, and Japheth. The name Ham means "dark or black," Shem means "dusky or olive-colored," and Japheth means "bright or fair." Biblical scholars, and at least one prominent anthropologist, consider Ham to be the ancestral father of Negroes, Mongoloids and Indians; Shem is considered to be the ancestral father of Semites (Arabic and Jewish); and Japheth is considered to be the ancestral father of Caucasians." (16)

"Observation: History can be divided into three dimensions. Generally speaking, each race has been given 2000 years to reign: the Reign of Ham – 4000 B.C. to 2000 B.C.; the Reign of Shem – 2000 B.C. to 300 B.C.; and the reign of Japheth – 300 B.C. to the present. What will happen when Japheth's reign is over? Could it be that we then enter into a period that I call the Reign of Jesus?" (34)

What God revealed to me was that all mankind is wicked and no matter whose descendants have ruled the earth, white or black, they all did evil in the eyes of the Lord (Ecclesiastes 7:20). The struggle is not between black people and white people but it is between good and evil.

Men and women of the world are no more than puppets whose strings are pulled by spiritual forces in high places. Each person will have to examine their own heart and decide who they are going to allow to pull their strings, either God or Satan.

God is not the cause of evil. Despite the wickedness that is taking place in the world, God still sent His Son to die for our sins to give us the opportunity to be saved and restore our broken relationship with Him.

Even prior to receiving this revelation from God, my father echoed this same truth. One day I came to him complaining about the white supervisors that I worked for and I told him that I wanted to work for black people; I figured that at least that way I would get a fair shake.

My father explained to me that the issue is not about working for white people or black people but it is learning to work with people's personalities. He told me that there are good white people and there are bad white people. There are good black people and there are bad black people and that I need to learn how to discern whether the person themselves are good or bad.

He finally told me that if I walk through life expecting all white people to treat me bad and all black people to treat me well, then I will set myself up for failure because there are some white people who are going to be just as instrumental in helping me achieve success in life; as well as some black people. Furthermore, there will be just as many black people trying to tear me down as well as white people. It's not about black and white, but good and evil.

Blessings in the Trauma

Are You A Dumb Kid?

[14]The teaching of the wise is a fountain of life, to turn aside from the snares of death. (NASB) –Proverbs 13:14

As I mentioned before, my high school administrator Dr. Sullivan, had every opportunity to kick me out of school but he saw something in me and he pushed me to perform at a higher level. In my junior year, he struck a nerve when he brought me into his office and challenged me by asking me if I was a dumb kid. I was so pissed off with him that I actually started doing my work and made the honor roll for the first three quarters of the school year. I didn't make it the last quarter because it started getting warm outside and I started hooking school.

Dr. Sullivan proved my dad's theory about white people because that white man is one of the main reasons I made it through high school. Dr. Sullivan I don't know if you will ever read this book but if you do, *'Thank You!"*

You're Fired!

[16]Fools have short fuses and explode all too quickly; the prudent quietly shrug off insults. (The Message) –Proverbs 12:16

When I got fired from my first job, I was severely depressed and ashamed of myself. I couldn't believe that I allowed myself to get baited in and lose my composure; which ended up costing me my job. The good thing was that since I was such an excellent worker, they allowed me to resign as opposed to being terminated.

Regardless of whether or not I felt like the white supervisor set me up and was out to get me, I still was wrong for losing my temper. Since then, I've learned how to manage my anger and not take everything so personal. There are proper ways to handle things and God had to show me that I can't go around trying to use fear and intimidation to solve my problems.

What worked in the streets, doesn't work in corporate America and I had to learn to play the game. Most importantly, I had to learn how to be a man and not throw a temper tantrum like a little child when something didn't go my way.

Ego Maniac Computer Tech

12He who despises his neighbor lacks sense, but a man of understanding keeps silent. (NASB) –Proverbs 11:12

Well, I got what I asked for when I worked as a computer technician for Egor, the black supervisor at the graduate library. This ended up being the worst job that I ever had. God always gives you an opportunity to retake a test that you failed because it took everything I had not to choke this man out. God allowed me to go through that experience to reinforce my father's point that it is not about black and white but good and evil, because this man had some serious demonic activity going on in his soul.

I just thank God that I was mature enough not to allow his critical comments to push me over the edge because if I would have given in, then I possibly would have been kicked out of school. I learned that sometimes it is just better to walk away and when you do, God will have something better waiting for you around the corner.

First Engineering Job

14"You shall not oppress a hired servant who is poor and needy, whether he is one of your countrymen or one of your aliens who is in your land in your towns. 15"You shall give him his wages on his day before the sun sets, for he is poor and sets his heart on it; so that he will not cry against you to the LORD and it become sin in you. (NASB) –Deuteronomy 24:14-15

The supervisor at my first engineering job definitely low-balled me regarding the starting salary that he offered me. I guess he figured that since I was fresh out of college, I would be desperate for a job and take whatever he threw at me. It wouldn't have been that bad but I knew that he offered me such a low starting salary because I was black.

Despite this apparent act of racism, one thing I learned from this incident is to know my worth and never let anyone devalue me. His offer was an insult and I thank God that He provided me with another job opportunity at a different engineering company.

What I also realized is that racism is spiritual and it is perpetuated by demonic influence. All white people are not racist but unfortunately this particular man suffered from racial prejudices. However, just like the amoebas that thrived after being subject to adverse conditions, racism actually caused me to push myself to be twice as good as my competition. What the enemy thought would break me God used to make me.

Glass Ceiling Profession

[11]Therefore they did set over them taskmasters to afflict them with their burdens. And they built for Pharaoh treasure cities, Pithom and Raamses. [12]But the more they afflicted them, the more they multiplied and grew. And they were grieved because of the children of Israel. [13]And the Egyptians made the children of Israel to serve with rigour: [14]And they made their lives bitter with hard bondage, in mortar, and in brick, and in all manner of service in the field: all their service, wherein they made them serve, was with rigour (ruthlessness). –Exodus 1:11-14

[4]Now to the one who works, his wage is not credited as a favor, but as what is due. (NASB) –Romans 4:4

[11]He who loves purity of heart and whose speech is gracious, the king is his friend. (NASB) –Proverbs 22:11

This experience really opened my eyes to the way the world really operates. My supervisor had me jumping through hoops, knowing that he was never going to pay me what I deserved. He just kept waving that carrot in my face and I just kept working harder and harder to get it not knowing that I would never be able to reach it. I still thank God for this job because I learned to persevere. The more hoops that he made me jump through, the harder I worked. The harder I worked, the more I built up my resolve to push myself to achieve my goals.

Again, this was another example of racism but I also have to take some of the blame because I never established any relationship with any of my coworkers outside of work. Even though I was a good worker, I isolated myself and no company will promote you if they feel that you are not a team player.

At the end of the day, we all have to play the game. I wasn't willing to play the game back then because I equated playing the game with selling out. There is a fine line between the two but playing the game is about building relationships and networking and selling out is about losing your identity to fit in. I've learned that you will never be successful in life unless you learn the skills of tact and diplomacy, which are crucial in building relationships.

In the end, God showed me that my life didn't revolve around engineering but Him. I learned a lot from the engineering profession that has served me well throughout my life and in other projects that I have been a part of. Therefore, I don't regret the time I put into getting my engineering degree. I also learned that my wealth is not going to come from working for somebody else's company but it is going to come from starting my own.

At one point in time, I was upset with my former employers for not compensating me according to my abilities. But now, I thank them for not paying me what I deserved because it just made me hungrier and more determined to seek God and fulfill my purpose and not settle for a salaried job.

Ultimately, it was not racism holding me back but God's divine intervention. God used different people (white and black) and circumstances to get me to grow in areas where I was deficient. I've learned to submit to God's will and let God use whatever people or circumstances (good or bad) He sees fit to mold me into who and what He wants me to be. He is the Potter and I am the clay (Jeremiah 18:6).

TRUTH

1. God is not to blame for the wickedness that is taking place in the world; but Satan is. Despite our sinful state God still sent His Son to die for us so that we could be saved.
2. The struggles that we are facing today are not caused by people, namely black and white people, but by spiritual wickedness in high places. People are just puppets but they

have to decide who will pull their strings, either God or Satan.

3. Never judge a person by their race or ethnicity but look at their heart because that will be the determining factor whether they are good or evil.

4. Don't let Corporate America or any person define your value or determine your future. God has a plan for your life and He will reveal it to you as you walk with Him.

5. You have to develop some level of tact and diplomacy in order to be successful in life because your prosperity is rooted in your ability to build healthy relationships.

6. God uses good and bad people and circumstances to mold you into who and what He wants you to be. His will overrides your will.

22

Life Lessons In Death

Luke 16:19-31 – [19]*"Now there was a rich man, and he habitually dressed in purple and fine linen, joyously living in splendor every day.* [20]*And a poor man named Lazarus was laid at his gate, covered with sores,* [21]*and longing to be fed with the crumbs which were falling from the rich man's table; besides, even the dogs were coming and licking his sores.* [22] *Now the poor man died and was carried away by the angels to Abraham's bosom; and the rich man also died and was buried.* [23] *In Hades he lifted up his eyes, being in torment, and saw Abraham far away and Lazarus in his bosom.* [24] *And he cried out and said, 'Father Abraham, have mercy on me, and send Lazarus so that he may dip the tip of his finger in water and cool off my tongue, for I am in agony in this flame.'* [25]*But Abraham said, 'Child, remember that during your life you received your good things, and likewise Lazarus bad things; but now he is being comforted here, and you are in agony.* [26] *And besides all this, between us and you there is a great chasm fixed, so that those who wish to come over from here to you will not be able, and that none may cross over from there to us.'* [27]*And he said, 'Then I beg you, father, that you send him to my father's house—* [28] *for I have five brothers—in order that he may warn them, so that they will not also come to this place of torment.'* [29] *But Abraham said, 'They have Moses and the Prophets; let them hear them.'* [30] *But he said, 'No, father Abraham, but if someone goes to them from the dead, they will repent!'* [31]*But he said to him, 'If they do not listen to Moses and the Prophets, they will not be persuaded even if someone rises from the dead.'" (NASB)*

In the Scripture above, there were two men; a rich man and a poor man named, Lazarus (not the same Lazarus that Jesus resurrected). Both men died and Lazarus went to heaven and the rich man went to hell, because he spent all of his wealth on himself.

After waking up in hell, he begged Father Abraham to send him back so that he could warn his brothers in hopes that they would repent of their sins and avoid being sent to hell to suffer as he was.

Father Abraham told him that if their hearts were so hardened that they wouldn't listen to Moses and the Prophets, then they wouldn't listen to anyone from the dead either.

When I was a child, I was terrified of death. This fear of death followed me into adulthood. I was scared to even look at people in caskets. It wasn't until my mother passed away that I actually touched a person in their casket. Her death gave me the courage to confront that fear.

I have since come to understand that the people who have passed away have a story to tell regarding how you should or shouldn't live your life. Death is a time to reflect on a person's life and seek ways in which you can improve your own. The man in the Scripture above wanted to go back and warn his brothers but it was too late.

Once someone has passed away it is too late for them to come back to instruct us on the proper ways to live but we can take the opportunity to reflect on their lives and learn from their victories and defeats. Once I understood this, it helped me to view death differently and gave me a healthier outlook on life. Then, I was able to reflect on the many funerals that I attended at an earlier age and learn from the lives of those that had gone before me.

2You learn more at a funeral than at a feast—After all, that's where we'll end up. We might discover something from it. (The Message) —Ecclesiastes 7:2

Blessings in the Trauma

The Back Room

34"Then the King will say to those on His right, 'Come, you who are blessed of My Father, inherit the kingdom prepared for you from the foundation of the world. 35'For I was hungry, and you gave Me something to eat; I was thirsty, and you gave Me something to drink; I was a stranger, and you invited Me in; 36naked, and you clothed Me; I was sick, and you visited Me; I was in prison, and you came to Me.' (NASB) —Matthew 25:34-36

As depressing as it was to see my Aunt Katie (my grandmother's sister) bedridden, I will never forget how my grandmother cared for her. I watched my grandmother bathe her, change her clothes and administer her medicine. Witnessing this act of hospitality by my grandmother impressed upon me the responsibility that we all have to serve those in need. This heart of service that was modeled before me by my grandmother is one of the reasons why I ended up working in full-time ministry.

Goodbye Granddad

12Let the deacons be the husbands of one wife, ruling their children and their own houses well. **−1 Timothy 3:12**

My grandfather was not a deacon but he was faithful to my grandmother and managed his household well. He was only in his mid-fifties when he died. Some of his kids hadn't reached adulthood when he passed; but all of his children made something out of their lives because of the example that he set.

If God ever blesses me with kids, I pray that I can set this type of example. Should I pass away before they reach adulthood, prayerfully I would have instilled enough godly principles in them so that in my absence they will still become successful and honor God with their lives.

Little Derrick

26In the fear of the LORD is strong confidence: and his children shall have a place of refuge. **−Proverbs 14:26**

I don't know the details of Derrick's death by drowning at that pool, but what God has shown me in this incident is that whenever children are in my care, I need to protect and provide for them at all times. Children are precious and we always need to make their safety our number one priority. The memory of Derrick's funeral and the cause of his death prompted me to be extremely vigilant as I ran the day-to-day operations of the Junkyard Kids Summer Camp. I also impressed upon the employees to be highly attentive and alert as they supervised the kids, especially during field trips.

As a kid, I also didn't know how to swim and didn't learn until I was a teenager. However, if God ever blesses me with kids, I will make sure that they receive swimming lessons as soon as they are able because incidents like the death of little Derrick can be prevented if parents take the proper precautions and provide their children the necessary training and education early on in life. Training and instructions serve as a refuge for your children, which can keep them safe from danger.

Uncle Lawrence

³²He that is slow to anger is better than the mighty; and he that ruleth his spirit than he that taketh a city. −Proverbs 16:32

I didn't know too much about my Uncle Lawrence except for the stories that my mother and father told me about him. At one point, I did become angry and violent like he was; but I thank God that I was able to change and get my anger under control. I don't know if Uncle Lawrence ever had the opportunity to get his anger in check; but I do know that God is merciful and all final judgments regarding a person's life are in His hands.

Uncle Jack

⁶And he shall turn the heart of the fathers to the children, and the heart of the children to their fathers, −Malachi 4:6a

My father didn't spend much time with me growing up so he saw funerals as an opportunity to take me to meet his family because funerals were one of the only times that our family got together. If my father would have been in tune with what was going on with me, he would have noticed that I was scared to death in that funeral home seeing all of those dead bodies and he would have shielded me from such an experience.

I know that being a parent isn't easy and everyone is prone to make mistakes but again, if God blesses me to have children, I will never expose them to so much death. I also will take them to meet and socialize with their relatives on a regular basis and during festive occasions, and not only during times of crisis or death. Children are precious and you have to be mindful that their early years are the most critical in the development of their self-esteem and confidence. Therefore, you have to protect them from experiencing things that can scar them for life.

Uncle Bo

6Train up a child in the way he should go: and when he is old, he will not depart from it. –Proverbs 22:6

My father and his siblings were raised on the rough streets of Baltimore, Maryland and many of my father's family members and friends were swallowed up in the street life and died before their time. This was the fate of Uncle Bo. I am proud of my father because he fought and made his way out of the projects of Baltimore and his tenacity and desire to become successful in life overshadowed his circumstances. God gave my father an indomitable spirit to fight his way through adversity and he passed this same spirit on to me.

Uncle Eddie

1A good name is rather to be chosen than great riches, and loving favour rather than silver and gold. –Proverbs 22:1

Uncle Eddie's funeral was held in the month of February during an ice storm but despite the harsh weather conditions, his funeral was packed. Everybody loved Uncle Eddie and they all came out to pay their respects to him. He always took the time to talk to us and give us advice. He became a surrogate grandfather to my cousins and I after our grandfather passed away. I hope that I can touch and inspire as many people as he did so when I pass people will be willing to drive through an ice storm to pay their respects to me. Uncle Eddie had a good name.

Madea

6I have planted, Apollos watered; but God gave the increase. 7So then neither is he that planteth any thing, neither he that watereth; but God that giveth the increase. 8Now he that planteth and he that watereth are one: and every man shall receive his own reward according to his own labour. —1 Corinthians 3:6-8

⁵For I am mindful of the sincere faith within you, which first dwelt in your grandmother Lois and your mother Eunice, and I am sure that it is in you as well. (NASB) —2 Timothy 1:5

My grandmother was the first person to sit me down and read the Bible to me. She was the one who kept everybody in church. She planted the seed of Christ in my heart. My mother watered it and God gave it the increase through my father getting saved.

Even though I went astray for a couple of years, I always was conscious of God and that is what kept me from going over the edge (Proverbs 22:6). Despite my grandmother's illness, she continued to cook Sunday dinner for the entire family; even when she was taking chemotherapy. She was a fighter. I come from a stock of fighters.

TRUTH

1. Death is not to be dreaded but it is a time of peace and reflection on life.
2. Death is not the end of life but the beginning of eternity. How you lived your life will determine where you spend eternity.
3. Once you die, it is too late to make corrections so it is best to live right while you still have breath.
4. Your life speaks about you long after you are gone and what it says is determined by how you lived. Your life will be a teacher to those you leave behind so make sure that you leave behind a legacy of greatness.

23

Character

Psalm 15:1-5 *–¹O LORD, who may abide in Your tent? Who may dwell on Your holy hill? ²He who walks with integrity, and works righteousness, And speaks truth in his heart. ³He does not slander with his tongue, Nor does evil to his neighbor, Nor takes up a reproach against his friend; ⁴In whose eyes a reprobate is despised, But who honors those who fear the LORD; He swears to his own hurt and does not change; ⁵He does not put out his money at interest, Nor does he take a bribe against the innocent. He who does these things will never be shaken. (NASB)*

Romans 5:2b-4 *– ²...and we exult in hope of the glory of God. ³And not only this, but we also exult in our tribulations, knowing that tribulation brings about perseverance; ⁴and perseverance, proven character; and proven character, hope; (NASB)*

One day, when I first began to volunteer at The Soul Factory, Deron walked by me and said, "What's up Fast Eddie?" After he said that I asked him, why he called me Fast Eddie and he replied by quoting Romans 4:17b, *"God calls things that are not as though they were."* I had seen the movie, *"The Hustler"* starring Paul Newman as Fast Eddie and Jackie Gleason as Minnesota Fats, so I had an idea of what he meant by his comment.

In the movie, *"The Hustler,"* Fast Eddie was a highly talented young pool shark who challenged the legendary Minnesota Fats, to a game of pool to determine which one of them was the best pool player. Minnesota Fats started off winning but after a while, Fast Eddie regained his confidence and began to beat Minnesota Fats convincingly.

After a while, they began to drink alcohol and Fast Eddie's game began to suffer. They played pool non-stop for two days straight and at the end of their duel Fast Eddie was drunk and beaten for all of his money. Minnesota Fats still looked sharp as if he hadn't even been in a grueling two-day pool competition and walked out of the pool hall with all of Fast Eddie's money.

Later on in the movie, Fast Eddie spoke to a gambler who was at the pool hall that had fronted Minnesota Fats the money to play him. The gambler told Fast Eddie that he had never seen anyone as talented at shooting pool as he was and he had also never seen anyone put Minnesota Fats on the ropes like he did. Fast Eddie asked him how did he end up losing if he was so talented and the gambler told him that he lost because he didn't have any character. He told Fast Eddie that talent means nothing if you don't have character.

When Deron called me Fast Eddie, I thought that he was saying that I didn't have any character. I got a little upset when he said that because I thought to myself, *"How is this man going to conclude that I don't have any character when he doesn't even know me?"* Later, I realized that he wasn't saying that I didn't have any character but that my character needed development.

So, the question is, *"What is character?"* According to Psalm 15, a few of the characteristics of godly character are: integrity, righteousness, truthfulness, kindness, loyalty, dependability, generosity, and honesty. The next question is, *"How does one develop character?"* The answer is found in Romans 5:2b-4, which states that *"suffering produces perseverance and perseverance produces character and character produces hope."*

The final question is, *"What is the purpose of developing character?"* That answer is found in Psalm 15:1, which states that only people with character can spend eternity with God, which is every Christian's hope. Character provides a person with stability and longevity. Only people with character ever achieve anything of great value or significance in life. Talent will get you through the door but character is what will help you to excel and achieve greatness. True character is what makes a person steadfast and indomitable. In the end, character is what will get you into heaven.

Diamonds and Clay

Diamonds are comprised of pure carbon that exists deep beneath the earth's surface. The deeper the carbon is placed beneath the earth's surface, the more heat the carbon will be exposed to. Over time, due to the extremely high temperatures and high pressure from the weight of the rocks and earth above, the pure carbon hardens and eventually forms a diamond. This is the same process that God takes every person through to develop their character.

God uses the pressures and trials of life to mold our character to reflect His because His whole goal is to transform us into His image (Colossians 3:9-10). I've concluded that every traumatic event that I experienced was just a test from God sent to develop my character. God is the master teacher and He will continue to teach and instruct us through trials and tribulation until He achieves His desired goal. God will never deliver us from our trials, but He will deliver us through our trials.

[1]The word which came to Jeremiah from the LORD, saying, [2]Arise, and go down to the potter's house, and there I will cause thee to hear my words. [3]Then I went down to the potter's house, and, behold, he wrought a work on the wheels. [4]And the vessel that he made of clay was marred in the hand of the potter: so he made it again another vessel, as seemed good to the potter to make it. [5]Then the word of the LORD came to me, saying, [6]O house of Israel, cannot I do with you as this potter? saith the LORD. Behold, as the clay is in the potter's hand, so are ye in mine hand, O house of Israel. –Jeremiah 18:1-6

Blessings in the Trauma

Kindergarten

[3]And said, Verily I say unto you, Except ye be converted, and become as little children, ye shall not enter into the kingdom of heaven. –Matthew 18:3

I started off as a timid and innocent child but because I grew up in such a hostile environment, I became angry, cynical and insecure. However, God used my environment to transform me from being timid to courageous. Now that the transformation is complete He has called me to return and become like that little child in kindergarten who was friendly and innocent. Over time, God has healed me and I am learning to become more loving, kind and compassionate again. Like a diamond, hard and indestructible but still precious and beautiful.

You Hurt My Knuckles

[10]Do not forsake your own friend or your father's friend, And do not go to your brother's house in the day of your calamity; Better is a neighbor who is near than a brother far away. (NASB)
–Proverbs 27:10

I don't know what possessed me to snitch on my friends in class that day but one thing I learned from this incident is never turn on your friends, especially just to get ahead. There will be times in your life where your friends will be all you have and according to the Scripture above, friends will be more valuable in times of trouble than your own family.

Loyalty is one of the most important virtues that you can have and without loyalty you will never develop true friendships. Without true friendships you will always be alone. If you're always alone then you will be destined for failure because God didn't design us to journey through life on our own. This was a painful lesson, one that my knuckles will never forget.

Shoe Box Design

[10]The thief cometh not, but for to steal, and to kill, and to destroy: I am come that they might have life, and that they might have it more abundantly. –John 10:10

I have always been self-motivated and creative but after that incident in the third grade when my classmates ridiculed me during my presentation, I became so intimidated that I stopped being creative. I realized that the enemy used events like this to steal my creativity and kill my desire to be different and try new things. When I reflect on that day, I am actually proud of myself because it took a lot of courage to do what I did. Most of the other kids wouldn't have even stood up and presented their project to the class but I pushed past my fear and did it.

God has put me in several situations where I've had no choice but to come out of my shell and face my fears. I've learned to trust my intuition again, which has led me to step out of my comfort zones and take more risk. Talent means nothing if you don't have the courage to use it. Successful people are trailblazers, not path-followers. Only people with willpower and faith can carry out their dreams during the day instead of fantasizing about them at night while they sleep.

But I Got the Ball

2When the battle is about to begin, let the priest come forward and speak to the troops. 3He'll say, "Attention, Israel. In a few minutes you're going to do battle with your enemies. Don't waver in resolve. Don't fear. Don't hesitate. Don't panic. 4GOD, your God, is right there with you, fighting with you against your enemies, fighting to win."... 8 The officers will then continue, "And is there a man here who is wavering in resolve and afraid? Let him go home right now so that he doesn't infect his fellows with his timidity and cowardly spirit."(The Message) –Deuteronomy 20:2-4, 8

The day Ms. Johnson's son's baseball landed on that frozen creek, I knew that whoever walked out there to get the ball would possibly fall through the ice but I figured somebody had to do it. Charlie and Harvey were too scared to go and get it but I wasn't.

Looking back, I see that on the surface I may have been timid at times but I had enough courage to rise to the occasion when necessary. Over the years, I have faced many instances like this where something unfortunate happened and everybody around me stepped down; but God gave me the courage to step up.

Baby Brother

12Therefore, strengthen the hands that are weak and the knees that are feeble, 13and make straight paths for your feet, so that the limb which is lame may not be put out of joint, but rather be healed. (NASB) –Hebrews 12:12-13

When my little brother was born, I came to a crossroad in my life. I made a decision to change and become somebody that he could respect and look up to. In order for me to gain his respect, I realized that I first had to gain respect from everyone else. His birth inspired me to become a fighter and begin to stand up for myself. He has since come to respect me and because he has learned from my mistakes, he has avoided many of the obstacles that I faced.

My mother told me that I am a leader and that people look up to me. Therefore, if I give up, then those who follow me will give up as well. No matter how weak you may feel somebody is looking to you for strength and inspiration and that should always be your motivation to never quit.

Too Small

27But God hath chosen the foolish things of the world to confound the wise; and God hath chosen the weak things of the world to confound the things which are mighty; –1 Corinthians 1:27

I recognize that even though my father said that I was too little to play football, that statement wasn't true. It was just an excuse that he made because he didn't want to take me to practice or the games because that would have required him to sacrifice too much of his time. Whatever the case, I learned that my size doesn't matter. If it has done anything, then it would be that my size has actually made me more courageous because I had to battle guys twice my size on a consistent basis.

It doesn't take any courage or fortitude to fight people smaller than you but it takes tremendous heart and courage to stand up to people bigger than you. God used all of those Goliath's I had to battle growing up to develop a warrior spirit within me because He was preparing me to face much bigger giants in the spiritual realm later in life. God always chooses the weak and lowly things of the world to accomplish His will because transforming underdogs into champions brings Him more glory.

Behind the Wall

25And in the fourth watch of the night Jesus went unto them, walking on the sea. 26And when the disciples saw him walking on the sea, they were troubled, saying, It is a spirit; and they cried out for fear. 27But straightway Jesus spake unto them, saying, Be of good cheer; it is I; be not afraid. 28And Peter answered him and said, Lord, if it be thou, bid me come unto thee on the water. 29And he said, Come. And when Peter was come down out of the ship, he walked on the water, to go to Jesus. –Matthew 14:25-29

I didn't throw any rocks at that school bus but I got blamed for it and called out by the bus driver and the kids on the bus. I was the smallest and youngest person out of the group of people that I was with but everyone on the school bus kept yelling and screaming my name. Eventually, I got so mad that my anger overcame my fear and I stood up for myself. I came from behind the wall on my own without following anyone else.

When the bus pulled off, I turned around to pick my book bag up off the ground and when I looked up all of the other kids were standing behind little 'ole me. These were the same people that used to beat me up. I stopped being scared of them after that. I realized that this event was the precursor for what God has planned for me. As I continue to face my fears and come from behind the wall of doubt and insecurity, I will inspire others to step out and do the same.

University of Maryland at College Park

[33]These things I have spoken unto you, that in me ye might have peace. In the world ye shall have tribulation: but be of good cheer; I have overcome the world. –John 16:33

The University of Maryland was a culture shock to me because I was never raised around white people and had no interaction with them on a regular basis. Furthermore, being the only black person in some of my classes also fueled my insecurities.

After about two years of being in the UMCP engineering program, I ran into a young lady at the local community college who had attended my high school. I told her that I was in the UMCP engineering program and she told me that her sister attended UMCP but dropped out because she couldn't handle the workload and transferred to another college.

Now people dropped out of UMCP all the time so that wasn't a big deal but what inspired me was in high school her sister was a straight "A" student and always maintained a 4.0 GPA. I believe she was even the valedictorian of our high school graduating class.

However, she couldn't handle UMCP. Ironically, the trouble maker who kept getting sent to the principal's office in high school was hanging in there and gutting it out in the UMCP engineering program. That was the day when God showed me that I was an overcomer. This brought me to tears.

I Surrender

[16]For God so loved the world, that he gave his only begotten Son, that whosoever believeth in him should not perish, but have everlasting life. –John 3:16

At this point in my life, I was dealing with some unbearable pain: my mom struggling with cancer, stuttering, my best friend sent to prison, grueling engineering program and a broken heart. So like my dad, I decided to give God a try and when I gave my life to Christ, He began to start working things out for me.

Looking back over my life, this was one of the toughest seasons that I've ever been through but in retrospect I realize that it was the best season because it brought me to God. Because God gave me the strength to endure that season I have had the confidence to face and overcome other challenges in my life as well.

Physics Tutorial Class

[22]The stone which the builders rejected has become the chief corner stone. (NASB) –Psalm 118:22

Physics was one of the hardest classes in the engineering program. I dreaded going to the physics labs and study classes because I was afraid to speak in front of people because of my stutter. Despite my fear, I kept going to my physics lab and the physics study classes because I needed all of the help that I could get to complete my homework assignments.

One day when I was in my physics lab, I asked one of my classmates to let me borrow his calculator and when I took the cover off I saw that he had the answers to the previous exam we had just taken taped on the inside cover of his calculator. Later on, I learned that many of the white students were cheating and some of them got the old exams and projects from their friends who had taken the classes before them. This boosted my confidence because here I was working hard, studying by myself still maintaining a "B" average and they had a network.

The following semester a couple of my friends formed a study group and I ended up being the leader and coordinator of the group. We kept this group together throughout our entire engineering curriculum. Then the unbelievable happened, a couple of the white students who were the brightest in our class would come to me periodically to compare their answers to the homework. They would also consult me whenever we had to complete engineering projects.

Wow, the stutterer, who people laughed at, became known as the one who had the answers because I studied diligently day and night and never quit. This was when I realized that I wasn't inferior to white people and my confidence was elevated.

Library Front Desk

[12]*and we toil, working with our own hands; when we are reviled, we bless; when we are persecuted, we endure;* [13]*when we are slandered, we try to conciliate (reconcile); (NASB)*
–1 Corinthians 4:12-13a

Working the front desk at the library was terrifying because this was my first customer service job and I was always nervous about stuttering. I constantly focused on stuttering, which caused me too stutter. Some people didn't notice it, but others did and they would laugh at me and one lady even made fun of me one day.

I hated working at the front desk but I made up my mind not to run from it. Sometimes, I even volunteered for the front desk because I knew that was a fear I had to conquer. Some days were better than others but I learned that I had the resolve and strength to persevere. The front desk was a battlefield for me but I survived. It was on this battlefield that I learned to endure the criticism of people and still be courteous and professional.

Suicidal Interview

[37]Nay, in all these things we are more than conquerors through him that loved us. **–Romans 8:37**

After I humiliated myself during my first engineering interview, I seriously contemplated killing myself. The main reason I didn't go through with committing suicide was I knew that my mother didn't have long to live and my father was already in his sixties. This meant that in the future, there wouldn't be anyone around to help support my younger brother.

So, I pushed through and overcame for him. I've learned that in life if you are just living for yourself, then that is not enough motivation to push you to overcome your struggles but living to help somebody else will motivate and inspire you to overcome your challenges. Knowing that someone is depending on you gives you the strength to persevere. This is true love and love is the greatest motivator in the world.

Sahid

[15]Study to show thyself approved unto God, a workman that needeth not be ashamed, rightly dividing the word of truth.
–2 Timothy 2:15

[15]But sanctify the Lord God in your hearts: and be ready always to give an answer to every man that asketh you a reason of the hope that is in you with meekness and fear: **–1 Peter 3:15**

*[1]For the Law, since it has only a shadow of the good things to come and not the very form of things, can never, by the same sacrifices which they offer continually year by year, make perfect those who draw near. [2]Otherwise, would they not have ceased to be offered, because the worshipers, having once been cleansed, would no longer have had consciousness of sins? [3]But in those sacrifices there is a reminder of sins year by year. [4]**For it is impossible for the blood of bulls and goats to take away sins**. [5]Therefore, when He (Jesus Christ) comes into the world, He says,*

"SACRIFICE AND OFFERING YOU HAVE NOT DESIRED, BUT A BODY YOU HAVE PREPARED FOR ME; [6] *IN WHOLE BURNT OFFERINGS AND sacrifices FOR SIN YOU HAVE TAKEN NO PLEASURE.* [7] *"THEN I SAID, 'BEHOLD, I HAVE COME (IN THE SCROLL OF THE BOOK IT IS WRITTEN OF ME) TO DO YOUR WILL, O GOD.'"*

[8]*After saying above, "SACRIFICES AND OFFERINGS AND WHOLE BURNT OFFERINGS AND sacrifices FOR SIN YOU HAVE NOT DESIRED, NOR HAVE YOU TAKEN PLEASURE in them" (which are offered according to the Law),* [9] *then He said, "BEHOLD, I HAVE COME TO DO YOUR WILL." He takes away the first in order to establish the second.* [10]*By this will we have been sanctified through the offering of the body of Jesus Christ once for all.* [11]*Every priest stands daily ministering and offering time after time the same sacrifices, which can never take away sins;* [12] *but He (Jesus Christ), having offered one sacrifice for sins for all time, SAT DOWN AT THE RIGHT HAND OF GOD, (NASB)*
—Hebrews 10:1-12

When I first met Sahid, I had just given my life to Christ so I wasn't grounded in God's Word. After meeting with Sahid, I contemplated becoming a Muslim, especially after reading his paper about Islam versus Christianity. I sought help from my father and my pastor at the time but they couldn't help me so I prayed to God and He answered my prayer by telling me to study. After hearing that, I went and bought a Study Bible and downloaded several Bible commentaries offline.

I began to dissect the paper that Sahid gave me. In time, I was able to address every comment he made and refute it with Scripture. After a while, I realized that what he was saying didn't make any sense to me and that his arguments weren't credible. I then wrote a paper to counter his paper and met with him to discuss my findings.

Sahid, as well as other Muslims believe in the Old Testament, especially the first five books of the Bible. So in our meeting I asked him if he believed that the people in the days of Moses gave animals to be sacrificed for their sins and he said yes. Then I asked him why Muslims don't continue to give animal sacrifices to God to atone for their sins. I then told him that Christians don't because

Jesus Christ was the final sacrifice for our sins and faith in Him and His shed blood on the cross cleanses us upon our confession.

I then shared with him that if he didn't believe that Jesus Christ was the only begotten Son of God who took away the sins of the world through His shed blood and death on the cross then he should still be giving animal sacrifices to atone for his sins. He responded by saying that they still give sacrifices but not necessarily blood sacrifices. I then said only blood can atone for sin and nothing else. Sahid had no answer and that was the end of the meeting.

After our meeting Sahid told me, "Terrence you're not going to convert me and I'm not going to convert you so let's just leave it alone." Later on that day when I walked across the parking lot to my car, I started crying again but this time they were tears of joy. I began to thank God because I realized that He sent Sahid to me so that I would buckle down and study His Word; which ultimately brought me closer to Him. My soul had been anchored.

College Graduation

[13]I can do all things through Christ which strengtheneth me.
–Philippians 4:13

I remember taking my very first engineering class at UMCP, which was Introduction to Engineering. This course combined all of the engineering students from the various engineering disciplines; civil, mechanical, electrical and environmental. On the first day of class, the Dean of the Engineering Program addressed the students. At that time it was over five hundred students in the auditorium. He said in four to five years, when it is time for this class to graduate, more than half of the students will have dropped out of the program and switched majors because not everybody has what it takes to survive the engineering program.

Well by the grace of God, I survived and made it through the UMCP Clark School of Engineering Program. I endured stuttering in the lab classes, stuttering working at the front desk of the library, being ridiculed by my classmates, having a verbally abusive supervisor, overnight study sessions, a strenuous engineering curriculum, and many nights of anxiety to graduate with a 3.33

GPA from the University of Maryland at College Park with a Bachelor's of Science Degree in Civil Engineering.

This is a pretty impressive accomplishment to have on any resume. The funny thing is that you don't even use eighty-five percent of what you learn in college in your career field. The college curriculum's main focus is not only to prepare you for your profession but to prepare you for life. If you can make it through any science or engineering program at any major university, then you can make it through anything. Instead of a Bachelor's of Science Degree in Civil Engineering, my degree should have read Bachelor's of Science Degree in Character.

What also made this day special was seeing my mother in the audience. She had survived to see me walk across the stage again. She was one of the main reasons that I made it. I was really thankful that God allowed her to see it because I believe that moment helped to overshadow all of the stress I had ever put her through. She is a real example of true character.

More Bad News

*[32]And what more shall I say? For time will fail me if I tell of Gideon, Barak, Samson, Jephthah, of David and Samuel and the prophets, [33]who by faith conquered kingdoms, performed acts of righteousness, obtained promises, shut the mouths of lions, [34]quenched the power of fire, escaped the edge of the sword, **from weakness were made strong**, became mighty in war, put foreign armies to flight. (NASB) –Hebrews 11:32-34*

On the week that my mother died, I had just undergone reconstructive knee surgery and I found out that my ex-girlfriend had a baby two months prior. I couldn't believe it. I felt like God was trying to kill me. The pain from all three of these incidents was unbearable. I had no plans of getting back with my ex-girlfriend but after losing my mother and having my ACL rebuilt, news like that just added fuel to the fire.

However, after being encouraged by my Aunt Tricia, I prayed and asked God to give me the strength to stand because I knew that my family depended on me. If I folded, then they were going to fold as well. As soon as I finished that prayer, I was empowered. I put my crutches in my closet and started using a cane because I was determined to walk on my own two feet at my mother's funeral instead of hobbling around on a pair of crutches.

There were several people I hadn't seen in years that came and attended my mother's funeral. One of my friends who I used to run the streets and get into trouble with was in attendance as well as his parents. His father approached me after the funeral and said that he was extremely proud of me for the man I had become and he wanted me to talk to his son for him because he hoped that whatever God had done with me would rub off on his son.

That comment really inspired me because it helped me to see that I was a changed man and that God had turned my most painful and weakest moment into an opportunity to display great resolve and strength, for His glory. God showed me that although I used a cane to walk around at my mother's funeral, the one thing that really provided the support for me to stand and not fold under the pressure and pain that I was dealing with was my character. God had been developing my character through my trials and tribulations for that very moment.

TRUTH

1. Only people with character can dwell in eternity with God.
2. Talent will get you an opportunity but character will get you to the top.
3. Character, like diamonds, is formed under intense heat and pressure.
4. God's main purpose for our lives is to transform us so our character mirrors His.
5. Every trial and test that you experience is sent from God to develop your character

24

Evergreen

Acts 16:16-26 – [16]*And it came to pass, as we went to prayer, a certain damsel possessed with a spirit of divination met us, which brought her masters much gain by soothsaying:* [17]*The same followed Paul and us, and cried, saying, These men are the servants of the most high God, which shew unto us the way of salvation.* [18]*And this did she many days. But Paul, being grieved, turned and said to the spirit, I command thee in the name of Jesus Christ to come out of her. And he came out the same hour.* [19]*And when her masters saw that the hope of their gains was gone, they caught Paul and Silas, and drew them into the marketplace unto the rulers,* [20]*And brought them to the magistrates, saying, These men, being Jews, do exceedingly trouble our city,* [21]*And teach customs, which are not lawful for us to receive, neither to observe, being Romans.* [22]*And the multitude rose up together against them: and the magistrates rent off their clothes, and commanded to beat them.* [23]*And when they had laid many stripes upon them, they cast them into prison, charging the jailor to keep them safely:* [24]*Who, having received such a charge, thrust them into the inner prison, and made their feet fast in the stocks.* [25]*And at midnight Paul and Silas prayed, and sang praises unto God: and the prisoners heard them.* [26]*And suddenly there was a great earthquake, so that the foundations of the prison were shaken: and immediately all the doors were opened, and every one's bands were loosed.*

Romans 8:16-18 – [16]*The Spirit itself beareth witness with our spirit, that we are the children of God:* [17]*And if children, then heirs; heirs of God, and joint-heirs with Christ; if so be that we suffer with him, that we may be also glorified together.* [18]*For I reckon that the sufferings of this present time are not worthy to be compared with the glory which shall be revealed in us.*

An evergreen is a tree that can stay green all year long. It never sheds it leaves and despite the weather; spring, summer, fall or winter, it continues to grow. Its survival is not dictated by the elements but by its own ability to sustain itself. Unlike deciduous trees that require a lot of nutrients and energy, which they pull from the earth, evergreens do not require as many nutrients and can replenish the limited nutrients that they pull from the soil within themselves.

During the colder seasons of the year, deciduous trees have to shed their leaves because they cannot absorb as many nutrients from the ground to sustain their foliage; only enough to sustain their trunk and branches. However, evergreen foliage provides insulation for the tree which prevents sun and frost damage to the trunk and branches. The foliage on most evergreens conserves water, which helps to reduce the amount of evaporation through the leaves. Evergreens are nature's truest examples of prospering even in rough times.

My mother was a spiritual evergreen. Despite her ongoing battle with cancer and the strenuous cancer treatments, she never lost her faith in God. It is one thing to praise God when things are going well but when you can still praise God in the midst of a storm, speaks volumes about your faith. She never felt sorry for herself or complained about her situation but she continued to praise and honor God, which kept everyone around her uplifted.

Although my father played a major role in her courageous stand against cancer, my mother was able to go to God on her own behalf and pull the power that she needed whenever her circumstances got rough. When you can praise God while you are in the furnace of affliction, God releases power to break the bondage off of other people; similar to the story told in Acts 16:16-26, when Paul and Silas praised God after they were beaten and God shook the jail house and set the prisoners free.

That is why I am still here today because my mother praised God while she was receiving chemotherapy and radiation treatments and He honored her by breaking the chains off of her son. She was able to endure because she considered that her present sufferings were not to be compared to spending eternity with Christ.

Blessings in the Trauma

Ma, What's Wrong?

³Energize the limp hands, strengthen the rubbery knees. ⁴Tell fearful souls, "Courage! Take heart! God is here, right here, on his way to put things right and redress all wrongs. He's on his way! He'll save you!" (The Message) **–Isaiah 35:3-4**

At the surface level, my mother was extremely reserved and insecure but deep down, in the pit of her soul, was a tenacious fighter. As a child, I would see her sitting around the house depressed a lot because her marriage was suffering, she didn't like her job and she missed her family in Memphis, Tennessee.

It seemed as though the woman who had braved the waters at just twenty years of age; who moved from a small southern town to a fast-paced metropolitan district without her family, had been lost. However, never judge a book by its cover and God has a way of bringing what is lying dormant inside of a person out of them through their trials.

Bad News

¹⁹Woe is me, because of my injury! My wound is incurable but I said, "Truly this is a sickness, and I must bear it."(NASB) **–Jeremiah 10:19**

When my mother was diagnosed with cancer in 1992, I thought that the world was going to end. However, what we thought was bad news for us really turned out to be worse news for the enemy. On that very day, my mother prayed and God gave her a resolve like no other. Her mind was made up to fight cancer tooth and nail. No one would have fathomed in a thousand years that she was going to survive another ten years with cancer and during the course of that time, hundreds of people would have their faith in God strengthened and renewed, especially mine. God used one woman's illness to heal many.

One Handed Bandit

[1] They that trust in the LORD shall be as mount Zion, which cannot be removed, but abideth for ever. **–Psalm 125:1**

When the doctors removed the lymph nodes from my mother's neck and accidentally cut some of the nerves to her left arm and hand, she just took it in stride. I was severely upset but my mother didn't let it get her down. She would just keep moving her fingers and balling her hand into a fist to keep her hand from going numb. I realize that this fist symbolized her fight.

She was like a hurdle runner in the Olympics that runs full speed then leaps over the hurdles in front of them. The only thing different about my mother's race was it seemed as though as she jumped a hurdle, the next one would be even higher. The more hurdles she jumped, the higher they got and instead of complaining she just ran harder and jumped higher. No matter what obstacles were placed in her way, her faith and trust in God could not be shaken and with one hand she cooked the best Thanksgiving Dinner's I've ever had.

Pick Your Head Up

[32] And I, if I be lifted up from the earth, will draw all men unto me. **–John 12:32**

People always tuned in whenever my mother gave a testimony because they knew that she was going through a lot of pain and suffering and it amazed them how someone could still praise God while going through such adverse circumstances. As I began to cry one day at Bible Study while she was giving a testimony, my father told me to pick my head up.

It didn't register to me then why he told me that but now I understand. You never feel sorry or pity someone who is suffering on account of serving Christ because it is disrespectful. When you can praise God despite your circumstances, it lifts Christ up and inspires other people to fight and not give in to their trials. Testimonies about the goodness of God while you are still in the storm draw people to Him because they realize that you are riding on His supernatural power and everyone wants to experience that level of power.

In Luke 23:27-28, when Jesus was carrying His cross on His way to be crucified, the women followed behind and were crying and he told them *"Don't weep for me, but weep for yourselves."* Similarly, my mother didn't like pity and wouldn't stand for anyone feeling sorry for her because she knew that ultimately her sickness brought glory to God.

God is Good

[1]Praise ye the LORD. O give thanks unto the LORD; for he is good: for his mercy endureth for ever. –Psalm 106:1

On the day that my mother had that surgery and her lungs collapsed, I began to lose faith in God. That's why she looked at me and wrote on the paper, *"God is good."* Later on, she told me that God told her that she didn't need to get the operation and that she wasn't going to lose her voice but she allowed the doctors to put fear in her, which led her to disobey God. She said that she was just happy that God spared her life and if she had to walk around with a tube in her throat to breathe for a little while, then so be it because ultimately what mattered most was God had given her more time to be with her family. God is good!

Bloody T-Shirts

[6]God said, "All right. Go ahead—you can do what you like with him. But mind you, don't kill him." [7]Satan left God and struck Job with terrible sores. Job was ulcers and scabs from head to foot. [8]They itched and oozed so badly that he took a piece of broken pottery to scrape himself, then went and sat on a trash heap, among the ashes. [9]His wife said, "Still holding on to your precious integrity, are you? Curse God and be done with it!" [10]He told her, "You're talking like an empty-headed fool. We take the good days from God—why not also the bad days?" Not once through all this did Job sin. He said nothing against God. (The Message) –Job 2:6-10

Seeing my mother wake up in the morning with those bloody t-shirts on was a horrific sight. I just could not understand why God was allowing her to experience so much suffering. Then one day, she told me that she felt like Job and what she realized was that if she could accept good things from God, then she should also be able to accept bad things as well. It was this attitude that kept her from cursing God and falling into depression. So my father continued to help her change her bandages and dress her wounds. During that season they just kept extra t-shirts by the bed at night.

I Look Like A Monster

[8]For we would not, brethren, have you ignorant of our trouble which came to us in Asia, that we were pressed out of measure, above strength, insomuch that we despaired even of life: [9]But we had the sentence of death in ourselves, that we should not trust in ourselves, but in God which raiseth the dead: –2 Corinthians 1:8-9

The only time I saw my mother break down was when she developed that infection that caused her face to swell so much that her facial features were barely recognizable. Again, episodes like this caused me to get angrier and angrier with God but during this time my father stepped up even further and comforted my mother.

In the end, God sustained her and she was able to endure this too and remain steadfast in her faith. It seemed to me that the enemy was throwing everything he had at my mother but now I understand why. If he could have made her fold, then many other people would have folded as well. Several people were looking up to her because they knew that she was one of God's elect.

This is My Cross

[24]Then said Jesus unto his disciples, If any man will come after me, let him deny himself, and take up his cross, and follow me. –Matthew 16:24

God doesn't throw pity parties and He doesn't attend them either because He knows that He has something waiting for us in eternity that far outweighs our current troubles. My mother understood this truth and that is why she told me to leave her alone when she was in the bathroom every morning coughing up the bile and mucus that developed in her lungs as she slept at night.

She knew that all followers of Christ are given a cross to bear and that cancer was the cross that Christ had given to her. I believe that she didn't want me to pity her because she was setting an example for me not to ever seek pity and to endure whatever circumstances that may come my way like a good soldier of Christ, no matter what (2 Timothy 2:3).

Let Me Dress You

[13]And one of the elders answered, saying unto me, What are these which are arrayed in white robes? and whence came they? [14]And I said unto him, Sir, thou knowest. And he said to me, These are they which came out of great tribulation, and have washed their robes, and made them white in the blood of the Lamb.
–Revelation 7:13-14

The day when my mother and I were sitting at the table eating and she told me about her dream, where a man came to her dressed in all white and took off her old clothes and put all new white clothes on her like his clothing, was her way of telling me that she didn't have much longer to live. That dream was proof that God was pleased with her and that He had been with her every step of the way. Later on, that dream comforted me because I realized that when she passed away she went straight to heaven. One day, she told me never to forget her and I thought to myself, *"How in the world could I ever forget my hero?"*

2002 Women's Day Conference

*[8]"Now be ye not stiffnecked, as your fathers were, but **yield** yourselves unto the LORD, and enter into his sanctuary, which he hath sanctified for ever: and serve the LORD your God, that the fierceness of his wrath may turn away from you."*
–2 Chronicles 30:8

My mother worked long and hard preparing that speech for the Women's Day Conference. She spoke on the letter *"Y"* from the word *"Unity"* and from the letter *"Y"* she chose the word *"Y.I.E.L.D."* The following is a summation of her speech and the meaning of the acronym *"Y.I.E.L.D."*

❖ **Yes** – *When God calls you to serve Him, respond by saying, "Yes Lord, send Me."*

❖ **Invite** – *When God knocks at your heart, always be prepared to invite Him in.*

❖ **Endure** – *As you endure your hardships, you become a more effective witness for Christ.*

❖ **Love** – *Love one another because God is love and He sent His only begotten Son to die for us.*

❖ **Doers** – *Let us not just be hearers of the Word but doers, so that we can spread the Gospel.*

To this day, I cannot watch the video of my mother's speech without crying. My counselor Dr. Betty told me that although my mother gave this speech at the Women's Day Conference; ultimately, it was really a message that God had her leave for me. I hear you Mama, and know that I have yielded.

No More Pain

[4]And God shall wipe away all tears from their eyes; and there shall be no more death, neither sorrow, nor crying, neither shall there be any more pain: for the former things are passed away.
–Revelation 21:4

On the day that my mother passed away, it seemed to me like the world just stopped moving and that everything was motionless. When I finally arrived at the hospital that night and saw my mother lying lifeless on that hospital bed, it felt like someone stuck a dagger into my heart. I cried for a while but then I just began to stare at her and notice how peaceful she looked. She looked as if she were asleep.

I hadn't seen her sleep that peaceful in years without coughing and tossing and turning in bed. She was finally at peace and there was no more pain. It was selfish of me to want her life to continue with all of the pain that she was going through but seeing her lying there with her eyes closed gave me a peace because I knew that she was finally at rest. Although my father, my brother, and I were in that hospital room staring at her body in mourning, she was in heaven standing next to Christ staring down at us saying, *"I'm fine now because although I am absent from the body I am present with the Lord."(2 Corinthians 5:8)*

Well Done Mama

[15]Precious in the sight of the LORD is the death of his saints.
—Psalm 116:15

[13]And regarding the question, friends, that has come up about what happens to those already dead and buried, we don't want you in the dark any longer. First off, you must not carry on over them like people who have nothing to look forward to, as if the grave were the last word. [14]Since Jesus died and broke loose from the grave, God will most certainly bring back to life those who died in Jesus. (The Message) —1 Thessalonians 4:13-14

There wasn't much grieving at my mother's funeral because there was no doubt in everybody's mind that she was in heaven. The Pastor titled my mother's eulogy, *"A First Class Ticket Into Heaven"* because she was such a valiant fighter.

On the day that she passed away, I pictured, in my mind, as she first stepped foot into heaven that there were seven angels standing at the gates who gave her the twenty-one gun salute announcing the entrance of another soldier joining the Lord's army in heaven.

Once she walked through, she bowed down at Jesus' feet and then He said, *"Well done Betty Jones, My good and faithful servant, you have been faithful over a few things, now I will make you ruler over many things. Enter now into the joys of thy Lord."* (Matthew 25:21). When we buried my mother, a piece of me was buried with her but I was comforted because I knew that I will see her again; for one day very soon we will meet together with Christ in the air (1 Thessalonians 4:13-17).

My Only Friend

[13] "As one whom his mother comforts, so I will comfort you; And you will be comforted in Jerusalem." (NASB) **–Isaiah 66:13**

[37] He that loveth father or mother more than me is not worthy of me: and he that loveth son or daughter more than me is not worthy of me. **–Matthew 10:37**

Growing up, I wasn't as close to anyone like I was to my mother. She was first and everybody else was a distant second. She was my best friend and I could tell her anything. We went out to the movies and dinner together and we really enjoyed each other's company. To see her suffer from cancer in front of my eyes knowing that there was nothing that I could do to help her caused me to become embittered with God.

She really resented that and she always told me to never let go of my faith because God has always provided for me and that He has had a special hedge of protection around me to preserve my life. I have since repented to God for my feelings toward Him regarding my mother and He showed me that although my mother truly loved and cared for me, there was no one who loves and has cared for me as much as He has.

God ultimately is my Mother and my Father and I have come to learn that no one should ever take His place in my life. I just thank God for having provided me with such a spiritual and loving mother who led me to Him.

God has and always will provide for His people and in the absence of my mother God has put several women in my life who have given me motherly wisdom and guidance namely; my mother's youngest sister, Aunt Patricia, Deron's wife and Co-Pastor of The Soul Factory, Jill Cloud, and last but not least Dr. Betty, my spiritual counselor.

I knew that my life crossing paths with Dr. Betty was divine intervention because her full name is Dr. Betty Williams and my mother's maiden name was Betty Williamson. I don't believe in coincidences but God orchestrated this because he knew that Dr. Betty would help me navigate through my trauma and see the blessings in my pain, which would ultimately help me to overcome my past hurts and carry out my destiny.

TRUTH

1. If you can't praise and worship God in your storms then your praise isn't worth much.
2. God doesn't throw pity parties and He expects everyone to bear their cross like Jesus did.
3. The sufferings of this world don't compare to the joys of spending eternity with Christ.
4. Those who die in Christ, immediately upon their deaths, enter heaven to be with Him.
5. No one should ever take God's place in your life. He must always come first.
6. God feels your pain and He will provide whenever you lose a loved one.
7. Life must go on for you after the death of your loved ones because you still have a purpose to fulfill.

25

My Crown

Matthew 27:28-29a – *[28]And they stripped him, and put on him a scarlet robe. [29]And when they had platted (twisted) a **crown of thorns**, they put it upon his head,*

Luke 8:7, 14 *–"Other seed fell among the thorns; and the thorns grew up with it and choked it out. [14]"The seed which fell among the thorns, these are the ones who have heard (the Word of God), and as they go on their way they are choked with worries and riches and pleasures of this life, and bring no fruit to maturity. (NASB)*

Maslow's Hierarchy of Needs Diagram

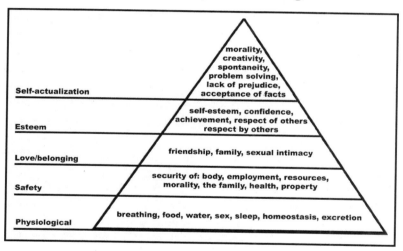

(**Note**: Information for diagram taken from Wikipedia: The Free Encyclopedia.)

Abraham Maslow was an American psychologist who during the course of his study of human behavior concluded that human beings have five basic needs that have to be met in order to achieve what he calls, *"peak performance"* or high points in life. Those five basic needs are: physiological, safety, love/belonging, esteem and self-actualization. He further explains that one cannot ascend to the highest level of basic needs, which is self-actualization, until all needs below it are met. Each need listed on the pyramid cannot be met until the need below it is fulfilled.

After being introduced to Maslow's Hierarchy of Needs by a friend of mine in college, I then began to evaluate my life to determine what level of the five basic needs I lined up with on the diagram. I came to the conclusion that I was only at the second level of the diagram, which is safety and could not ascend to love/belonging, esteem and self-actualization.

Due to the resentment I built up towards my father, seeing my mother suffer from cancer and being raised in a hostile community, I was unable to really experience love or a sense of belonging. It wasn't until I started going to counseling and confronting the issues of my past that I was able to begin my ascent up the pyramid with hopes of reaching a level of *"peak performance,"* which is equivalent to fulfilling your destiny.

Maslow's Hierarchy of Needs is an excellent tool to use to evaluate one's psychological well being but ultimately the path to true self-actualization is found only in God. In Matthew 27:28-29, the soldiers mocked Jesus by placing a crown of thorns on top of His head, not realizing that the crown of thorns actually validated His authority as the King of kings and Lord of lords.

This crown once pressed upon His head caused Him great agony and pain as blood poured down His face. It was that very blood that cleansed mankind of our sins. At this point, Jesus was about to fulfill His purpose by being lifted up on the cross; thus, drawing all men unto Him. The crown of thorns symbolized the pain and suffering one has to endure to achieve their destiny in life. It was this very crown that distinguished Jesus from the two thieves, one to His left and the other to His right, and caused everyone to focus their attention on Him. After Christ gave His life on the cross the sky was darkened and the earth quaked, then even his crucifiers confessed that He was the Son of God.

I was exposed to God's Word at a very early age in life and proceeded to attend church well into my teenage years but the worries of life choked the Word of God out of me. I allowed the thorns in my life and the pursuit of sinful pleasures to cause me to distance myself from God instead of allowing the pain from the thorns to draw me closer to God. It wasn't until I received true spiritual guidance and counsel that I was able to reflect on my life and understand that God used my thorns to prick my soul and allow all of the poison from my sins to drain out of my spirit.

God's ultimate plan is for His Spirit to train our spirits to guide our lives, which will enable us to carry out His will. Proverbs 25:2 says, *"It is the glory of God to conceal a thing: but the honour of kings is to search out a matter"* and God has revealed to me that the matter that the king has to search out is his own past and discover that all of the trials and tribulations that he has endured served to prepare him to receive authority from God to conquer his own God-given destiny.

Once a king accepts this truth and makes peace with the trauma in his past, he can then endure the pain from the crown of thorns that God has placed on his head with dignity and honor.

Blessings in the Trauma

Pneumonia

[15]The king of Egypt had a talk with the two Hebrew midwives; one was named Shiphrah and the other Puah. [16] He said, "When you deliver the Hebrew women, look at the sex of the baby. If it's a boy, kill him; if it's a girl, let her live." (The Message) –Exodus 1:15-16

I am in no way comparing myself to Moses; however, for the first couple of years of my life I had to box with death. I spent the majority of my infancy in the hospital battling pneumonia. Pneumonia is not even a common illness known to my family, especially to the degree that I was suffering from it.

When I shared this information with my counselor, Dr. Betty, she said that God had a plan for me since I was born and the enemy knows that God plans to use me in a special way. So, he has been on assignment to take me out and he started long ago, right after I was born. She said that I have been in a fight for my life since day one and I need not worry about death because I won't leave this earth until my mission is complete.

Reverend Ronald McDonald

[8]I am the LORD: that is my name: and my glory will I not give to another, neither my praise to graven images. *–Isaiah 42:8*

As embarrassing as this event was for me in the second grade, one thing it did was it impressed upon me the importance of a leader to be humble and sacrificial. My father was real upset about this assignment because he felt that the person who was the focal point of the assignment was what he called, a *"glory hound."* My father defined a *"glory hound"* as a person who performs acts of service, not necessarily to provide for the needs of the people but to promote their own status and selfish agenda.

God has shown me that whenever I commit myself to carrying out His will, that all glory and honor should be given to Him and Him only. None of it should be accredited to me. As long as I can remain humble, God can continue to elevate me. The moment I become arrogant or prideful is the point of self-elevation and from that point is where He will bring me down.

Dr. King

[8]Also I heard the voice of the Lord, saying, Whom shall I send, and who will go for us? Then said I, Here am I; send me. *–Isaiah 6:8*

After watching that movie about Dr. King, then talking to my father as he explained all that Dr. King had done for our people, I became really inspired and wanted to help people as he did. I was only seven years old but God used that movie to plant that desire to uplift people in my heart.

As I've grown and become a man, God has watered that seed to the point where I chose to follow Him, which caused me to walk away from engineering and real estate and be lead by my internal compass which directed me to serve His people. I continue to pray to God that He continues to give me the courage to follow the desires of my heart and always be ready to move when He calls.

Field Day

[10]Yes, give me wisdom and knowledge as I come and go among this people—for who on his own is capable of leading these, your glorious people?" (The Message) –2 Chronicles 1:10

As my team and I walked off of the field on Field Day, I felt like a loser because it appeared to me that we weren't going to win anything and I wouldn't receive any awards to show my dad so that he could be proud of me. On the day of the awards ceremony, I just slumped in my seat with my arms folded. As they began to go down the list and call out the awards for each event, all I heard was, *"First place winners are Terrence Jones' team, come on down!"* I was shocked and at the end of the day my team had won just about every award.

This was the very first time I was assigned to lead a group of people and because I wanted to make my natural father proud of me, I reached deep down inside of myself and pushed my team to victory. I realized that God orchestrated that event to inspire me and to let me know that I was a born leader.

That same desire I had to perform well and make my natural father proud is the same desire and drive I need to persevere and make my Spiritual Father proud as well. This experience helped me truly understand that individual accomplishments are great but achieving success as a team is better. This reminds me of a quote by veteran IRL Indy Car Series team owner, Ron Hemelgarn:

> *"Success is not measured by how high you climb but by how many people you can bring with you."*

Get Off Me

[5]"And whoever receives one such child in My name receives Me; [6]but whoever causes one of these little ones who believe in Me to stumble, it would be better for him to have a heavy millstone hung around his neck, and to be drowned in the depth of the sea. (NASB) –Matthew 18:5-6

When I was a child, I didn't realize that what Ms. Wesley's daughters did to me could be considered molestation because they never performed any sexual acts on me nor did they force me to perform any sexual acts on them. However, I learned later that molestation isn't just a sexual act but it is any act where someone is forcing their will on another person without that person's consent, especially if the weaker individual is a child.

This experience combined with the fact that I was already withdrawn caused me to become repelled by intimacy. When I got older and began to deal with females, I would have sex with them but I couldn't acquire any feelings for them or show them any affection. I could never just hold a woman, caress a woman, or even be gentle with a woman. It was strictly sex with no emotional attachments on my part.

Again, sex outside of marriage is forbidden and I don't condone the sexual acts that I had with women prior to my days of abstinence. However, I'm referring to them to show that what I experienced at Ms. Wesley's as a child hindered me in developing healthy relationships with women in adulthood.

The ultimate lesson from this incident is to never allow someone to watch your kids if you haven't done your homework on them first. Before you ever agree for anyone to watch your children, you must interview them. I would even venture to say interrogate them this way you will put the fear of God in them. This will enable you to get all pertinent information to ensure that you are leaving your children in good hands.

The early stages of your child's life are the most critical in their development and incidents like what I experienced could drastically damage their psyche for the rest of their lives. If it is God's will for my life, one day I will have children and if I do I will do everything in my power to provide an environment where they will be nurtured and protected.

I would never allow anyone, family members or friends, to spend time with my kids without my supervision if I had the slightest inclination that they would do my children any harm. I also wouldn't be concerned about hurting their feelings by my decision to supervise their time with my kids because my children's spiritual and emotional well being would be more important to me than their feelings being hurt. God gave me the strength to overcome molestation to ensure that I will guard my kids or any other children left in my care with my life.

I'm Walking

¹⁴Multitudes, multitudes in the valley of decision: for the day of the LORD is near in the valley of decision. –Joel 3:14

My mother's fear of me walking home by myself after school caused her to continue to put me in daycares that were abusive and traumatizing. She didn't know what was going on because I was too afraid to tell her but after a while I couldn't take it anymore and I had to take a stand for myself.

Sometimes God stirs up our circumstances to get us to move. Life oscillates, one minute you're on the mountaintop and the next minute you're in the valley. Unfortunately, many of us won't move and do what God tells us to do until we encounter His judgment in the valley. There are two things I learned from this incident: 1) Don't take on other people's fear and make them your own and 2) Learn how to make up your own mind and stand on what you believe.

I knew what was best for me at that time even though I was only eleven years old and I couldn't allow my mother's fears to keep me in those daycares. I always seek wisdom and advice before I make any decision, especially life-changing decisions. However, I've learned that I can't expect other people to make decisions for me and in the end I'm responsible for my own life. Therefore, all final decisions concerning my life will have to be made by me as I'm led by God.

I've always had my own mind and because of this I was able to break away from the crowd and do my own thing whenever I sensed the crowd was headed in the wrong direction. This is what makes you a leader, having the courage to do what you believe in even when others don't. I don't follow the crowd but oftentimes the crowd tends to follow me because I've learned how to make hard decisions and walk my own path.

What's Happening to Me?

[10]And Moses said unto the LORD, O my LORD, I am not eloquent, neither heretofore, nor since thou hast spoken unto thy servant: but I am slow of speech, and of a slow tongue. [11]And the LORD said unto him, Who hath made man's mouth? or who maketh the dumb, or deaf, or the seeing, or the blind? have not I the LORD? [12]Now therefore go, and I will be with thy mouth, and teach thee what thou shalt say. –Exodus 4:10-12

*[7]Because of the surpassing greatness of the revelations, for this reason, to keep me from exalting myself, there was given me a thorn in the flesh, a messenger of Satan to torment me--to keep me from exalting myself! [8]Concerning this I implored (begged) the Lord three times that it might leave me. [9]And He has said to me, "**My grace is sufficient for you, for (My) power is perfected in (your) weakness** " Most gladly, therefore, I will rather boast about my weaknesses, so that the power of Christ may dwell in me. [10]Therefore I am well content with weaknesses, with insults, with distresses, with persecutions, with difficulties, for Christ's sake; for when I am weak, then I am strong. (NASB) –2 Corinthians 12:7-10*

Out of all of the accomplishments and victories I have achieved in my life, there is one thing that I have not been able to master and that is stuttering. By the grace of God, I have endured many trials but this thorn by far has caused me the most pain. I have pleaded with God on several occasions to remove it as the Apostle Paul did pertaining to his thorn, and like the Apostle Paul, so far God has given me the same answer and that is; *"His grace is sufficient to keep me and His strength is made perfect in my weakness."*

Although stuttering is extremely embarrassing for me, I no longer allow it to hinder me from achieving my goals in life. I've also learned that there are several people who have stuttered and many others who currently stutter. Despite their stutter, they continue to excel. Moses was one of the greatest prophets in the history of the world and he stuttered so that lets me know that God can still do great things with me.

God has also shown me that He has allowed me to stutter to keep me humble, which also keeps me close to Him. So I thank God that

He cares enough about me to allow something in my life to keep me close to Him. I will gladly accept this thorn in my crown because despite the pain, God used it to help mold me into the man that I am today.

TRUTH

1. True self-actualization is only achieved through an ongoing relationship with God.
2. Your weaknesses are not meant to be hidden but exposed so that God can exhibit His strength in your weaknesses and ultimately bring glory to Himself.
3. God uses your thorns to form your crown. What you thought was your shame, really symbolizes your reign.

Epilogue

At one point in time, I was losing in the game of life because my mind had been conditioned to focus on failure and defeat as a result of the traumatic events I experienced. Despite my pessimistic mindset, I still had the fortitude to survive but I didn't have the courage to live. When I say, "live," I mean to stop being passive and take the initiative to lay hold of the things that God had planted in my heart instead of being shackled by the lies the enemy had planted in my mind.

It wasn't until I prayed to God for deliverance that He sent spiritual advisors into my life that helped me to dissect my past and see how God used my unfortunate circumstances to form me into what He desires me to be. God used every stone that the enemy threw at me to build a wall to protect and preserve my soul and fortify my spirit. Through prayer, counseling, fasting and studying God's Word, God transformed my mind and allowed me to begin to focus on the good in all circumstances as opposed to the bad. This new mindset caused me to stop blaming God for my misfortunes and to stop seeing God as my enemy but instead to view God as my Savior and Deliverer.

I've learned that life is not fair and if you're looking to be justified and repaid for the hell you have experienced then you will be searching for something that you will never find here on earth. What you need to look for instead is understanding. Understanding will allow you to make sense of your ups and downs and give you the strength to endure them, which will also empower others to conquer their challenges as well.

Some of the answers that we seek to some of the horrendous things that we have experienced will only be given to us when we get to heaven. You don't have to like it but you do have to accept it if you plan to walk with God. In the meantime, we just have to trust God with the outcome.

The purpose of the trauma that God allows into your life is to impregnate you with a vision that will grow in the womb of your heart and once your character is developed this vision will be birthed into your purpose. Many people are wandering through life trying to determine what they are called to do and what I've found is that your calling is connected to your greatest pain and your greatest fear. God allows pain and fear into our lives because through His power He transforms our pain into compassion and our fear into courage. When you add these virtues together, compassion and courage, they equal your purpose.

In the movie, *"Batman Begins,"* as a child, Bruce Wayne fell down a well and was attacked by bats. Later on, he witnessed his parent's murder in a back alley after leaving an opera. Due to the traumatic event of seeing his parents gunned down in the street, he had developed a desire to fight for justice and combat crime in Gotham City. The very thing that he was terrified of is what he adopted as his symbol for justice; bats. Now I know that *"Batman"* is a fictitious story, but the principle is sound.

Similarly, due to my traumatic upbringing and strained relationship with my father, I developed a strong desire to mentor and train troubled young boys and men, especially those who lacked the guidance and discipline of a father. God used the trials in my life to help me develop my talents of administration, supervision, problem-solving and leadership to assist me in carrying out the desire He put in my heart to develop and institute programs for the enrichment of at-risk youth and men who are struggling to succeed in life.

I am grateful to God because He has blessed me with many talents but the gifts that He has given me are writing and teaching, which I can only perform as I stay connected to Him. These two gifts require me to do the very thing that I've always feared doing, which is public speaking.

Now, why would God call you to do what you are afraid to do? The answer that God gave to me is that the fear of what you are called to do will keep you humble because it will keep you seeking and relying on God instead of relying on your own strength and ingenuity. This is why God would allow me to stutter, so whenever I get up to teach I will have humbled myself beforehand and in doing so, God would then give me the power to speak only what He would have me to say because He can trust that I will not seek glory for myself.

I still get nervous before I have to teach and speak publicly and I realize that it may always be a struggle. However, God has shown me that as people continue to witness me slay this Goliath they will receive the courage and strength to go and slay their own.

When Christ was resurrected from the dead on the third day after His death on the cross He appeared to His disciples in His resurrection body. Although He had a new glorious body, He still had the scars from His crucifixion. This was evident when He appeared to His disciples and said to Thomas in John 20:27, *"Put forth your finger and see my hands, and put your finger in my side."* These scars were His badges of honor. Isaiah 53:5b says, *"...by his stripes (wounds) we are healed."* Christ' blood which poured from His wounds is what purchased our salvation.

I believe that my mother is in heaven with Christ and she still has the scars on her chest from the boils caused by the skin cancer and the scar on her throat from the tracheotomy. I also believe that they won't look like they did when she was here on earth but they will sparkle like precious stones because they will testify to her struggle and how they were used to bring God glory.

Our scars are our badges of honor as well and we have to learn to see them that way so we can stop hiding them and expose them to the world as Christ did. Your pain and suffering properly displayed to the world will win souls for the kingdom of God. I had to learn to stop hiding the fact that I stuttered and be brave enough to say what I wanted to say whenever I needed to say it. There are times when I still stutter and people react differently, some laugh and some frown but despite how people respond I've learned not to let other people's words or opinions define me because God defines me.

Most people have no idea the amount of courage and sacrifice it takes to speak to an audience of people knowing that you stutter but God knows and as a result if I continue to follow His lead He will reward me accordingly. I'm a king in the earth and God used the trials that I have been through to fashion my crown but the biggest thorn by far that sits at the center of my crown is stuttering. Although the pain and shame from stuttering can be great at times, the power and glory of God is greater and this is what gives me the strength to march on.

Prayerfully, something was said in the pages of this book that touched your soul and helped to transform your mind to see God in everything and not to see defeat in anything. God wants to use you but first you have to be willing to be used. Your prosperity is buried in your pain, but the question is, are you willing to dig through your past to find it? I know you can and I know you will because your future depends on it.

I may never get a chance to meet you here on earth but prayerfully we will meet in heaven. When you get there just be on the lookout for two angels praising God in paradise and as you see them talking one of them may possibly have a scar on their throat and the other one, from time-to-time, may stutter.

Works Cited

Books

Carlson, M.D., Dwight L. *Overcoming Hurts & Anger: Finding Freedom from Negative Emotions.* Eugene, Oregon: Harvest House Publishers. 2000.

Chandler, Steve. *Reinventing Yourself: How to Become the Person You've Always Wanted to Be.* Franklin Lakes, New Jersey: Career Press. 2005.

Cloud, Deron. *How To Love A Black Man?* Atlanta, Georgia: Soul Factory Press. 2006.

Colbert, M.D., Don. *Deadly Emotions: Understand the Mind-Body-Spirit Connection That Can Heal or Destroy You.* Nashville, Tennessee: Thomas Nelson Publishers. 2003.

De Angelis, Ph.D., Barbara. *Confidence: Finding It and Living It.* Carlsbad, California: Hay House, Inc. 2005.

Forward, Ph.D., Susan. *Toxic Parents: Overcoming Their Hurtful Legacy and Reclaiming Your Life.* New York, New York: Bantam Books. 1989.

Hardy, Kenneth V. & Laszloffy, Tracey A. *Teens Who Hurt: Clinical Interventions to Break the Cycle of Adolescent Violence.* New York, New York: The Guilford Press. 2005.

Hendricks, Arlene. *Gems In The Coal Bin: Bringing Treasure Out of Trauma.* Boonville, California: GEMS Ministries. 1997.

McKissic, Sr., William Dwight. *Beyond Roots: In Search Of Blacks In the Bible.* Wenonah, New Jersey: Renaissance Productions, Inc. 1990.

Miller, Alice. *The Drama Of The Gifted Child: The Search for the True Self.* New York, New York: Basic Books. 1997.

Myers, Edward. *When Parents Die: A Guide for Adults.* New York, New York: Penguin Books. 1997.

Staff. *Random House Webster's College Dictionary.* New York, New York. Random House, Inc. 1997.

Music

Shakur, Tupac. *Dear Mama.* Me Against The World. Interscope Records, Atlantic. Feb. 1995.

Online Postings

Brotherson, Sean. *Understanding Brain Development in Young Children.* NDSU Extension Service. April 2005. Web Site: http://www.ag.ndsu.edu/pubs/yf/famsci/fs609w.htm

Dodge, Darrell M. *Stuttering: Basic Information.* The Veils of Stuttering. 26 Mar. 2009. Web Site: http://www.veilsofstuttering.com/basicinfo.html

Staff. *Your Child-Childhood Trauma and Its Effects.* American of Child and Adolescent Psychiatry. 2009. Web Site: http://www.aacap.org/cs/root/publication_store/your_child_childhood_trauma_and_its_effects

Williamson, Elizabeth. *Brain Immaturity Could Explain Teen Crash Rate.* The Washington Post. 1 Feb. 2005. Page A01. Web Site: http://www.washingtonpost.com/wp-dyn/articles/A52687-2005Jan31.html